LIFE IS

Delicious

A COLLECTION OF RECIPES FROM THE
HINSDALE JUNIOR WOMAN'S CLUB

LIFE IS *Delicious*

A COLLECTION OF RECIPES FROM THE HINSDALE JUNIOR WOMAN'S CLUB

This cookbook is a collection of favorite recipes, which are not necessarily original recipes.

Published by
The Hinsdale Junior Woman's Club

Copyright © 2007
The Hinsdale Junior Woman's Club
P. O. Box 152
Hinsdale, IL 60521
www.hjwc.us
1-800-517-HJWC

Cookbook photography generously contributed by
Diane Smutny, © DMS Photography 630-887-1050,
www.dmsphotography.com, diane@dmsphotography.com

Cookbook graphic design concepts generously contributed
by Christine Minnella

Library of Congress Control Number: 2007923726

ISBN: 978-0-9792152-0-9

Edited, Designed, and Manufactured by
Favorite Recipes® Press
An imprint of

FRP.

P. O. Box 305142
Nashville, Tennessee 37230
1-800-358-0560

Art Director: Steve Newman
Book Designer: Starletta Polster
Project Editor: Susan Larson

Manufactured in China

First Printing 2007   5,000 copies

Hinsdale Junior Woman's Club is a community service organization that strives to enrich our community, the lives of our members, and their families. HJWC's mission is to offer members a network of resources and opportunities; and serve as a leader of volunteer and philanthropic service.

Proceeds from the sale of this cookbook will be reinvested in the community through the Hinsdale Junior Woman's Club.

Contents

Foreword

There is no doubt that life is precious and each moment should be cherished, from a surprise snow day to the birth of a new baby. What better way to create lasting memories than with family, friends, and traditions built around food.

LIFE IS *Delicious* is a collection of favorite recipes from the Hinsdale Junior Woman's Club. These are the dishes that we prepare in our homes for our families and friends. Some of the recipes have been passed down for generations. Others are culinary creations by our club members. And others were graciously contributed by our friends. All of the recipes, and the memories that inspire them, are delicious.

LIFE IS *Delicious* is also a celebration of life in our quaint suburban villages, which encompass Hinsdale, Western Springs, Clarendon Hills, LaGrange, Oak Brook and Burr Ridge. Our towns, with their tree-lined streets, picket fences and large parks, lie only about fifteen miles outside the Chicago Loop with its skyscrapers and bustling activity. Only a century ago this was the country, with farmers settling and building towns around the newly constructed Chicago, Burlington & Quincy Railroad jetting out from the city — the same train line that now takes busy commuters to their jobs each day. Although we are not immune to the pressures of modern life, this remains a community where the local grocer knows you by name and friends come together to help a neighbor in need. We have the best of both worlds — the charm and comfort of a "small town" coupled with the sophistication that proximity to metropolitan Chicago brings. Here, life is delicious, indeed.

We invite you to take time to stop and enjoy the people that make your life special. Invite them to your table and cook up some lasting memories, celebrating that . . . Life IS Delicious!

—*The 2006–2007 Cookbook Committee*

Acknowledgments

MAJOR CONTRIBUTORS

We would like to extend a heartfelt thank you to our major contributors for their support of LIFE IS *Delicious*.

Turano Baking Company — Generous Sponsor of the Soups & Salads Chapter

Cookbook Photographer — Diane Smutny, DMS Photography

Graphic Designer for Cookbook Concepts — Christine Minnella

Food Stylists — Beth Buzogany, Pat Wichmann and Jamie Wichmann

Florist — Jane Gavran, Jane's Blue Iris Ltd., Floral Consultants

A special thank you to the families that graciously opened up their homes for our photo shoots.

Suzi and Roy Houff   *Heidi and David Keeling*
Megan and Tom McCleary   *Claudine and Chris Schramko*

COOKBOOK DEVELOPMENT COMMITTEE

Committee Co-Chairs	*Committee Members*	Toni Gentleman
Megan McCleary	Devon Allen	Heidi Keeling
Shelly McMillin	Polly Ascher	Karen Novy
Jackie Paez-Goldman	Cathy Bjeldanes	Kathy Riddiford
	Jeanne Blauw	Margie Saran
	Martha Bratt	Claudine Schramko
	Angela Buikema	Lisa Seplak
	Joan Fitzgerald Clopton	Renee Turano Novelle
	Katie Eschenbach	Courtney Waters

The cookbook committee thanks our families, whose enthusiasm and support made this cookbook possible.
You make our lives delicious every day!

HJWC 2006–2007 EXECUTIVE BOARD OF DIRECTORS

Rosanne Cofoid	Melissa Ehret	Jackie Paez-Goldman
President	*Secretary*	*Nominating*
Cindy Klima	Carolyn Excell	Tracy Anderson
1st Vice President/President-Elect	*Treasurer*	*Past President 2005–2006*
Courtney Stach	Liz Gonzalez	
2nd Vice President/Membership	*Assistant Treasurer*	

About Hinsdale Junior Woman's Club

"WE STRIVE TO ENRICH OUR COMMUNITY."

Strongly devoted to volunteer and philanthropic service, Hinsdale Junior Woman's Club (HJWC) has been helping children and families in need since 1949. Although its mission has not changed since its founding just on the heels of World War II, the club has gone from raising $800 to purchase an obstetrical table at Hinsdale Hospital in 1949, to raising more than $400,000 for nearby Wellness House, a cancer support center, in 2005–2006. With more than 230 members, the group has been recognized as the largest junior club affiliated with the General Federation of Woman's Clubs (GFWC) in the United States.

In this cookbook, LIFE IS *Delicious*, we honor the many women who have served HJWC throughout its nearly sixty-year history. Through the years, HJWC members have sponsored both small- and large-scale events, all with one goal in mind: to raise funds to help support children and families, both inside and outside the community. In addition to raising large financial contributions, the women of HJWC have donated their time and effort through hands-on service projects to make life better for others. They have pulled weeds, planted flowers, cooked meals, held clothing drives, and helped the community in countless other ways. In the process, they have enjoyed some laughs and created friendships that have lasted a lifetime. HJWC has proven through more than half a century of commitment to service that women coming together for a higher cause can truly make a difference in the world.

On behalf of HJWC, we thank you for your support now and in the future. The net proceeds from the sale of this cookbook will aid in the continued efforts of HJWC and its partners. We graciously thank you for your contribution to our long-standing tradition of service.

FAMILY ★ COMMUNITY

HJWC

HINSDALE JUNIOR WOMAN'S CLUB

PAST BENEFICIARIES OF THE
Hinsdale Junior Woman's Club

American Heart Association

Bonaparte School for Mentally Handicapped Children

Center for Independence

Chicago Public Schools

Children's Aid Network

Children's Art Initiative

Children's Research Foundation

Chinmaya Mission (India and Sri Lanka)

DuPage Community Clinic

DuPage Humanitarian Service Project

Easter Seals DuPage

Edward Hines, Jr., VA Hospital

Family Shelter Service

Farm Club of Hinsdale

Giant Steps

Good News Community Kitchen

Greater DuPage MYMs

Gus Foundation/Children's Memorial Hospital

Healing the Children

Heart Association of DuPage County

Heifer International

Hinsdale Community Service

Hinsdale Fire Department and Hinsdale Police Department (Firemen's Breakfast)

Hinsdale Hospital

Hinsdale Theatre

Hinsdale Youth Center

Hinsdale/Clarendon Hills Charity Classic

Hope for Homeless Families

Humanitarian Service Project

Illinois Fire & Safety Alliance

LADSE

LifeSource

Melding Young Moms

Onward Neighborhood House

Rochelle Lee Fund

Ronald McDonald House Charities

Share Your Soles

Soldiers Serving in Vietnam

St. Thomas Hospice

TLC Campers

Washington Square Retirement Community

Wellness House

Youth Employment Services

Sunday Brunch

CHERRY ALMOND BISCOTTI WITH COFFEE OR TEA 143

DOUBLE MELTED BANANA BREAD 134

SUNRISE BREAKFAST STRATA 153

PERFECT PANCAKES 145

FRESH FRUIT

ORANGE JUICE AND MIMOSAS

Inviting everyone over for brunch is one of the easiest and most satisfying ways to entertain. Whether you are celebrating Mother's Day or New Year's Day, a steaming pot of coffee, fresh flowers, and delicious food set the tone for a relaxing morning. Stacked glasses and carafes of juice placed on the kitchen island invite guests to gather round and help themselves while you flip pancakes. A silver tray of Champagne flutes filled with bubbly mimosas makes things even more festive. The stick-to-the-ribs goodness of the Sunrise Breakfast Strata will satisfy the heartiest of appetites. Warm up some maple syrup or whip up some fresh whipping cream for the Perfect Pancakes. For children, add some mini-chocolate chips to the pancake batter. They will love them! Your guests are sure to appreciate the delicious food and warm company.

Ladies Luncheon

FIG TART WITH GOAT CHEESE AND PROSCIUTTO 36

CREAMY MUSHROOM, POTATO AND LEEK SOUP 42

SWEET SPINACH AND STRAWBERRY POPPY SEED SALAD 49

LEMON TARRAGON CHICKEN SALAD SANDWICHES 59

APRICOT TEA BREAD 135

STUFFED STRAWBERRIES 106   LEMON SQUARES 128

PINK LADY MARTINIS OR CHAMPAGNE 22

When your best friend is facing a milestone birthday, honor her with a ladies luncheon. To make a memorable gift, send out scrapbook pages with the invitations, and ask your guests to decorate their pages with pictures and fond memories of the guest of honor. You can assemble the pages while everyone enjoys the Fig Tart and catches up with one another. Your best friend is sure to adore this one-of-a-kind gift filled with love. Once everyone has had a chance to chat and the scrapbook has been presented, it is time for lunch. After a lovely soup, the Lemon Tarragon Chicken Salad tastes heavenly on freshly baked croissants and is perfectly complemented by both the Spinach and Strawberry Salad and the Apricot Tea Bread. Luscious strawberries stuffed with sweetened chocolate chip cream and delicate Lemon Squares complete the meal. Your girlfriends won't be able to resist them, and the guest of honor won't have to blow out the candles.

Casual Meal with Friends

BAKED GOAT CHEESE 28

ITALIAN CHOPPED SALAD 54

HOMEMADE CRUSTY BREAD 141

TAGLIATELLE WITH PORCINI MUSHROOM PANCETTA SAUCE 84

CHOCOLATE SOUFFLÉ CAKES WITH CARAMEL SAUCE 116

Instead of going out with friends, why not ask them over to enjoy a casual evening at home? Serve dinner in your kitchen—the heart of the home. Don't be shy about asking your guests to chop vegetables or open a bottle of red wine. Your friends will feel like part of the family. When you sit down, the Baked Goat Cheese, with its melted cheese and fresh basil, will invite your guests to dig in. Bring out the Italian Chopped Salad and Tagliatelle in large bowls, and let them help themselves. While the plates are being cleared and the coffee is brewing, pop the Chocolate Soufflé Cakes in the oven and warm the Caramel Sauce. After dessert, you can pull out your old Scrabble game for some healthy competition, or simply linger and enjoy each other's company. Your friends will undoubtedly feel touched that you have opened up your home and your heart to them.

Elegant Entertaining

MUSHROOM TARTLETS 30

LEMON DILL SALMON ROLL-UPS 34

BUTTERNUT SQUASH SOUP 41

CRANBERRY WALDORF SALAD 52

BLUE CHEESE-STUFFED BEEF TENDERLOIN 75

ROASTED VEGETABLES 94

ICED LEMON CREAM AND BLACK RASPBERRY SAUCE 108

The holidays are the perfect time of year to host an elegant dinner party. Send engraved invitations. Set your dining room table with your finest crystal, china, and linens. Place the Lemon Dill Salmon Roll-Ups and Mushroom Tartlets on trays, ready to be passed during cocktails. Before your guests arrive, make sure to turn on some festive music to welcome them. After cocktails and appetizers by a roaring fire, move the party to your candlelit dining room. Your guests are sure to be impressed by the beautiful Blue Cheese-Stuffed Beef Tenderloin and Roasted Vegetables. Sit back and enjoy the compliments—you don't have to confess to them how simple they were to prepare! The Iced Lemon Cream is a delightfully refreshing way to end such a fulfilling meal. Fine food and wonderful friends are sure to make a memorable evening.

Fourth of July Barbecue

STACKED CAPRESE BITES 31

SHRIMP GAZPACHO 47

SWEET BASIL AND TOMATO CORN SALAD 55

HONEY-MARINATED GRILLED CHICKEN 66

POTATO SALAD 57

BERRY PIE 112

SANGRIA 20

Red, white, and blue abound on the Fourth of July, with flags flying from every home and throughout the village center. Crowds line the streets of Hinsdale for the annual old-fashioned parade. Little Leaguers and high school bands march, the fire engines' sirens blare, and children scramble for tossed candy. Create your own fireworks in your backyard with our Fourth of July menu. While you enjoy a glass of Sangria, watch the Stacked Caprese Bites fly off the platter. The salads complement the grilled chicken beautifully and will win rave reviews from your guests. The Berry Pie, with its red raspberries and blueberries, is a tasty and very patriotic dessert. After a satisfying meal, grab a blanket and head down to your local park to watch the sky light up with fireworks to celebrate our nation's birthday.

Football Party

SOUTHWESTERN BLACK BEAN SALSA WITH CHIPS 23

TORTILLA DIPPING BITES 32

BLACK BEAN CHILI 44

THREE-CHEESE DROP BISCUITS 142

CELEBRITY BROWNIES 126

ICE CREAM AND HOMEMADE HOT FUDGE SAUCE 109

College football sparks pride throughout our towns. With alumni from many of the top football schools living side-by-side, the rivalry can be fierce but is always in good fun. What better way to enjoy a football game than with a "tailgating" party? Have the Southwestern Black Bean Salsa and Tortilla Roll-Ups out and ready to snack on when your guests arrive, while the Black Bean Chili simmers in a slow cooker. For a fun finale, set up a brownie sundae bar with our Celebrity Brownies and vanilla ice cream. Put out an array of toppings, including whipped cream, colored sprinkles, candy bits, and hot fudge sauce. Rest assured, despite whoever wins on Saturday—Notre Dame, Michigan, Purdue, or Illinois—all of the neighborhood comes together on Sunday to cheer for the champion Chicago Bears!

DRINKS

&Appetizers

Photo: Southwestern Black Bean Salsa, Sangria

SANGRIA

This is strong, but delicious!

1 (1.5-liter) bottle of burgundy
1 cup vodka
1 cup brandy
1 cup Triple Sec
1/2 cup sugar
12/3 cups pineapple juice
12/3 cups cranberry juice
Sliced oranges, lemons and limes

Stir the burgundy, vodka, brandy, Triple Sec, sugar, pineapple juice and cranberry juice together in a pitcher. Garnish with the oranges, lemons and limes.

Yield: 13 (1-cup) servings

This recipe is pictured on page 19.

HISTORY—In October of 1949, the Junior Woman's Club of Hinsdale was formed under the sponsorship of Mrs. W. T. Dawson, president of the Woman's Club of Hinsdale. The club consisted of young mothers and career women who would meet once a month, on Friday evenings, at the Community House in Hinsdale. Miss Lee Cleary was elected president. A Spring Fashion Show and tea raised $800, which was used to purchase an obstetrical table for Hinsdale Hospital. Throughout its nearly sixty-year history, the women of the HJWC have donated their time, effort, and talents to enrich our community and assist others who are making a difference.

CHAMPAGNE-SOUTHERN COMFORT PUNCH

To make this delicious punch more festive, float an ice ring with lemon, lime, and orange slices in it.

2½ cups Southern Comfort
1 (2-liter) bottle lemon-lime soda
6 ounces frozen orange juice
    concentrate, thawed
6 ounces frozen lemonade
    concentrate, thawed

6 ounces lemon juice
Dash of sugar
1 bottle Champagne
Red food coloring

Stir the Southern Comfort, soda, orange juice, lemonade, lemon juice, sugar and Champagne together in a punch bowl. Stir in enough food coloring to make the punch the desired color.

Yield: 32 (½-cup) servings

STRAWBERRY SLUSH

½ cup pink lemonade drink mix
½ cup water
3 cups ice cubes

1½ cups fresh strawberries
Frozen nondairy whipped
    topping, thawed

Place the drink mix in a blender container. Add the water, ice cubes and strawberries. Process on high speed for 10 to 15 seconds. Stir and process for 5 seconds or until smooth. Spoon 1 to 2 tablespoons of whipped topping into each of four glasses. Pour the strawberry mixture over the topping.

You may add 1 shot of vodka to each drink for a summertime cocktail.

Yield: 4 servings

CITRUS MARTINI

This refreshing lemon and lime martini is served best when cold.

> 3 ounces Absolut Mandrin
> 1 ounce simple syrup (see sidebar below)
> 1½ ounces freshly squeezed orange juice
> Juice of ½ lemon
> Juice of ½ lime
> Ice

Combine the Absolut Mandrin, simple syrup, orange juice, lemon juice and lime juice in a martini mixer. Add enough ice to fill. Shake to combine and strain into a martini glass.

Yield: 1 martini

PINK LADY MARTINIS

> 2 cups cranberry juice
> 2 cups vanilla-flavored vodka
> 1 cup Chambord
> 1 cup heavy cream
> Raspberries

Combine the cranberry juice, vodka, Chambord and cream in a pitcher and stir to combine. Fill a cocktail shaker with ice. Add enough of the cranberry juice mixture to fill. Shake to combine. Strain into chilled cocktail glasses and garnish with raspberries. Repeat with the remaining cranberry juice mixture.

Yield: 8 martinis

SIMPLE SYRUP is a common ingredient in drink recipes. It's easy to make by boiling two parts sugar to one part water. Keep stirring until the sugar is fully dissolved and the combination thickens slightly; then let cool. For the Citrus Martini recipe, ½ cup sugar and ¼ cup water makes enough syrup for two martinis.

SOUTHWESTERN BLACK BEAN SALSA

This is also fabulous as a relish on grilled salmon or chicken.

1 yellow bell pepper, chopped
1 red bell pepper, chopped
1 (19-ounce) can black beans, rinsed and
    drained
1 red onion, chopped
1 tomato, seeded and chopped

Juice of 1 lime
1/2 teaspoon salt
1/2 teaspoon cumin
2 tablespoons olive oil
1/4 cup chopped fresh cilantro
1 small avocado, chopped

Combine the bell peppers, beans, onion, tomato, lime juice, salt, cumin, olive oil and cilantro in a bowl and mix well. Chill, covered, for 1 to 3 hours. Stir in the avocado and serve immediately. Serve with tortilla or pita chips.

Yield: About 4 1/2 cups

This recipe is pictured on page 19.

CORN SALSA

Salt to taste
3 large ears fresh corn
1 large tomato, finely chopped
1 (7-ounce) jar roasted sweet red peppers,
    drained and chopped
2 green onions, finely chopped
1 jalapeño chile, seeded and minced

3 tablespoons minced fresh cilantro
2 tablespoons freshly squeezed lime juice
1 tablespoon white wine vinegar
1/2 teaspoon salt
1/2 teaspoon pepper
1/4 teaspoon cumin
2 avocados, chopped (optional)

Bring enough water to cover the corn to a boil in a large saucepan. Add a small amount of salt and the corn. Cook for 3 minutes or until tender. Drain and immediately immerse in a bowl of ice water. Let stand until cool. Cut the kernels from the cobs. Combine the corn, tomato, red peppers, green onions, chile, cilantro, lime juice, vinegar, salt, pepper and cumin in a bowl and mix well. Chill, covered, for 2 hours or longer. Stir in the avocados and serve immediately. Serve with tortilla chips.

Yield: About 2 1/2 cups

GUACAMOLE

The Fruit Store's guacamole is a favorite amongst its loyal customers. Serve this with tortilla chips at your next party.

1 pound plum tomatoes, chopped
1 small onion, chopped
Juice of 1 lime
1 jalapeño or habanero chile, chopped
1 garlic clove, minced
1 tablespoon chopped cilantro
Salt and pepper to taste
3 medium to large avocados

Combine the tomatoes, onion, lime juice, chile, garlic, cilantro, salt and pepper in a bowl and mix well. Mash the avocados in a separate bowl. Add the avocados to the tomato mixture and mix well.

Yield: About 16 ounces

IN THIS DAY AND AGE of strip malls and national mega-stores, we are proud of the many small, local businesses that continue to thrive in our towns. There is a family-run bakery that has been baking wedding cakes and chocolate éclairs for more than fifty years, and a family-run grocery that has been in business since 1952. One of the oldest businesses in our community, the Fruit Store, traces its beginnings back to 1917, when August Serio delivered fruits and vegetables door-to-door to residents from a wagon pulled by his horse, Daisy.

In 1929, The Fruit Store opened in Western Springs. Later, another store was opened in Hinsdale. Things have changed quite a bit from the business' early days. The familiar Fruit Store truck has replaced Daisy, and pineapple is available year-round. However, owners Bob and Mick Yurchak and Al Enzbigilis take obvious pride in their store and maintain the qualities that have made the business a success for close to a century. The fruits, vegetables, and homemade foods are fresh and of the highest quality. The customer service is impeccable. When you walk into one of their stores, you feel as though you are being welcomed into a family.

FRESH GREEN HERB DIP

1 cup mayonnaise
1/2 cup sour cream
1/4 cup minced parsley
1/4 cup minced scallions

1 tablespoon white wine vinegar
1 tablespoon freshly squeezed lemon juice
Salt and pepper to taste

Combine the mayonnaise, sour cream, parsley, scallions, vinegar, lemon juice, salt and pepper in a bowl and mix well. Chill, covered, for 1 hour or longer. Serve with cold jumbo shrimp or vegetables.

Yield: About 2 cups

HOT CHILI TORTILLA DIP

1 (16-ounce) can chili beans, drained
1 pound ground beef
1/2 cup chopped onion

1/2 cup hot ketchup
2 1/2 teaspoons chili powder
1 cup shredded Cheddar cheese

Mash the beans in a bowl. Brown the ground beef with the onion in a saucepan over medium heat, stirring until the ground beef is crumbly; drain. Add the ketchup, chili powder and beans. Spoon into an ovenproof baking dish. Sprinkle with the cheese. Bake at 350 degrees for 10 minutes or until cheese is melted. Serve with tortilla chips.

Yield: About 28 (2-tablespoon) servings

BAKED CRAB DIP

16 ounces cream cheese,
  at room temperature
2 (6-ounce) cans flaked crab meat
2 tablespoons milk
1/4 teaspoon Worcestershire sauce

2 tablespoons pimentos
1/4 cup chopped onion
1/8 teaspoon garlic salt
1/2 cup sliced almonds

Combine the cream cheese, crab meat, milk, Worcestershire sauce, pimentos, onion and garlic salt in a bowl and mix well. Spread over the bottom of a 9-inch pie plate. Sprinkle the almonds over the top. Bake at 350 degrees for 30 minutes or until bubbly and golden brown. Serve hot with crackers.

Yield: 28 (2-tablespoon) servings

ARTICHOKE AND CHEESE SPREAD IN SOURDOUGH ROUND

1 (2-pound) round of sourdough bread
2 heads of garlic, minced
1 1/2 bunches of green onions, chopped
  (about 1/3 cup)
2 cups sour cream

8 ounces cream cheese, at room temperature
2 (14-ounce) cans artichoke hearts, drained
  and chopped
6 cups shredded Cheddar cheese
1 loaf cocktail rye bread

Cut the top off the bread and scoop out the bread, leaving a shell and reserving the bread for another use.

Combine the garlic, green onions, sour cream, cream cheese, artichoke hearts and cheese in a bowl and mix well. Spoon into the bread shell. Double wrap with heavy-duty foil and place on a baking sheet. Bake at 350 degrees for 4 hours. Serve with rye bread. The spread may also be baked in a baking dish.

Yield: 30 servings

BRANDIED BRIE

This delicious and easy appetizer comes from our 2006–2008 philanthropy's cookbook, Recipes for Success!
A Collection by The Center for Independence Through Conductive Education. *This is a wonderful recipe
to have at hand when unexpected guests arrive.*

¼ cup brandy	¼ cup (½ stick) butter
½ cup walnuts, chopped	½ cup packed brown sugar
½ cup pecans, chopped	Crisp apple slices
1 pound Brie cheese	Whole grain crackers

Pour the brandy over the walnuts and pecans in a bowl. Let stand for 2 hours. Remove the rind from the cheese
and discard. Break the cheese into pieces and arrange evenly in a small microwave-safe baking dish or serving dish.

Combine the butter and brown sugar in a bowl and mix well. Sprinkle over the cheese. Arrange the nuts attractively
over the brown sugar mixture. Microwave on medium power for 2 minutes or until the cheese is soft; do not melt.
Serve with apples slices and crackers.

You may substitute ¼ cup orange juice and ¼ teaspoon cinnamon for the brandy.

Yield: About 10 servings

THE HJWC HAS HAD THE PRIVILEGE of working with men and women who are
making a difference in the lives of others. The Center for Independence, which has been designated
as the primary philanthropy for HJWC's 2006–2008 club years, is a not-for-profit organization
founded by two determined parents, Patti and Chuck Herbst, who were committed to making the life of their son and the
lives of other children better. In the summer of 1996, Patti took her son, Justin, to a camp in Canada that was said to
help motor-disabled children through conductive education. Conductive education is an intensive method of teaching
children with motor disabilities to be more functionally independent. During the course of that summer, Justin learned to
take steps with a walker by himself—a step unimaginable before. The family returned home excited and hopeful.
However, traditional therapy available in the Chicago area was not sufficient and Justin's new-found skills began to fade
away. Through sheer determination, the Herbsts opened the Center for Conductive Education in the spring of 1999. By
teaching children with physical disabilities to independently walk, sit, dress, and eat, the Center has truly changed the
lives, dreams, and futures of numerous children.

BAKED GOAT CHEESE

1 (26-ounce) jar marinara sauce
1/4 teaspoon thyme
Salt and pepper to taste

1/4 cup chopped fresh basil
8 ounces goat cheese
1 loaf French bread, sliced

Heat the sauce in a saucepan over medium heat. Stir in the thyme, salt and pepper. Remove from the heat. Stir in the basil. Pour over the bottom of a shallow ovenproof serving dish. Cut the goat cheese into 1-inch thick rounds. Arrange over the sauce. Bake at 375 degrees for 10 minutes or until the cheese is softened and warm; do not melt. Serve warm with French bread.

Yield: 12 to 16 servings

MANGO CHUTNEY CREAM CHEESE SPREAD

1 (6-ounce) jar Old English cheese,
   at room temperature
8 ounces cream cheese, at room temperature
1 teaspoon curry powder

2 teaspoons white wine
4 ounces (about) Major Grey's Chutney with
   mango or chutney of choice
2 scallions, sliced

Combine the cheese, cream cheese, curry powder and wine in a bowl and mix well. Spread evenly on a serving dish to a depth of about one inch and allowing the edge of the serving dish to show on all sides. Spread the chutney over the top of the cheese mixture, allowing it to drip down the sides. Sprinkle the scallions over the top. Serve with crackers.

Yield: About 8 servings

PECAN-CRUSTED CHEESE BALL

8 ounces cream cheese, at room temperature
1 cup shredded Colby-Jack cheese
4 ounces deli ham, chopped
3/4 teaspoon garlic salt

3/4 teaspoon seasoned salt
1 tablespoon Worcestershire sauce
2 cups chopped pecans

Combine the cream cheese, cheese, ham, garlic salt, seasoned salt and Worcestershire sauce in a bowl and mix well. Shape into a ball. Roll in the pecans to coat. Serve with crackers.

Yield: About 10 servings

CORNED BEEF CROSTINI SPREAD

1 1/2 cups sour cream
1 1/2 cups mayonnaise
2 tablespoons minced onion
1 teaspoon dill weed

2 tablespoons dried parsley
1/3 pound deli corned beef, chopped
Crostini

Combine the sour cream, mayonnaise, onion, dill weed, parsley and corned beef in a bowl and mix well. Chill, covered, for 2 to 12 hours. Serve with crostini.

Yield: About 32 (2-tablespoon) servings

MUSHROOM TARTLETS

3 shallots, chopped
3 garlic cloves, minced
3 tablespoons butter
1 cup white mushrooms, finely chopped
1 cup portobello mushrooms, finely chopped
1 cup white wine

1 cup fresh flat-leaf parsley
1/2 cup whipping cream
Juice of 1/2 lemon
Salt and pepper to taste
2 packages frozen phyllo tartlet shells
(about 30 shells)

Sauté the shallots and garlic in the butter in a saucepan. Add the mushrooms and cook until all of the liquid has evaporated. Add the wine. Reduce the heat and simmer for 15 minutes or until almost all of the wine has evaporated. Stir in the parsley, whipping cream and lemon juice. Cook until heated through. Season with salt and pepper.

Let frozen shells stand for 10 minutes. Spoon the mushroom mixture into the shells. Place on a baking sheet. Bake at 350 degrees for 3 to 5 minutes.

Yield: 30 tartlets

SERVICE PROJECTS—In addition to fund-raising, HJWC assists numerous local organizations through hands-on service projects. These service projects have included everything from planting flower boxes (in the rain) to sponsoring book drives for underprivileged children. In the early 1950s, club members visited with patients at Hines Veterans Hospital each month and hosted bingo parties. The women sent care packages to soldiers during the Vietnam War. A commemorative blood drive was established in memory of those who lost their lives on September 11th. Over the years, the club members have provided breakfasts for local firefighters and police and organized numerous parties for those serviced by our various philanthropic partners—including a Christmas party for the families of Wellness House, a Day at the Zoo for the Gus Children, and a "kitchen shower" to benefit the Easter Seals of DuPage County.

STACKED CAPRESE BITES

One of our members created this recipe while trying to find a use for homegrown tomatoes and fresh basil that she had on hand. It's a fun twist on a classic caprese salad.

2 or 3 medium tomatoes, sliced
2 large fresh mozzarella balls, sliced
1/2 cup loosely packed basil leaves
8 slices sourdough or French bread

Garlic powder
Dried oregano
Salt and pepper to taste
4 tablespoons olive oil

Layer the tomato slices, mozzarella slices and basil leaves over each of four slices of bread. Sprinkle with garlic powder, oregano, salt and pepper. Top each with one of the remaining four slices of bread.

Brush a panini press with the olive oil and heat. Add one or two sandwiches and cook until brown on both sides. You may use a grill pan and place a heavy pan on top of the sandwich, turning once. Repeat with the remaining sandwiches. Cut into bites and serve warm with wooden picks.

Yield: 4 servings

TORTILLA DIPPING BITES

8 ounces cream cheese, at room temperature
1 cup sour cream
1 small can chopped green chiles, drained
3 green onions, sliced
4 ounces Cheddar cheese, shredded
1/2 teaspoon garlic powder
1 package (6-inch) flour tortillas
Tomato-based salsa

Combine the cream cheese, sour cream, chiles, green onions, cheese and garlic powder in a bowl and mix well. Spread evenly over the tortillas. Roll each tortilla up to enclose the filling. Chill until ready to serve.

Cut each rolled tortilla into bite-size pieces. Secure each piece with a wooden pick. Serve with salsa.

Yield: 18 servings

ANNUAL BENEFIT—Over the years, HJWC has raised over one million dollars for the benefit of numerous charities throughout the Chicago area. The annual fund-raising events have changed over the years—from elegant dinner dances to spring fashion shows to Texas Hold 'Em casino nights. Regardless of the type of event, they are always the highlight of the year and great fun! In recent years, the club has hosted a luncheon benefit that has attracted big national name speakers, like Stacy London from the hit TV cable series TLC's *What Not to Wear* in 2006 and Ted Allen, wine and food guru from *Queer Eye for the Straight Guy* in 2005. These two benefits alone raised over four hundred thousand dollars to benefit the club's chosen philanthropy.

SAVORY COCKTAIL MEATBALLS

2 pounds ground sirloin
3/4 cup dry bread crumbs
1/2 cup finely chopped onion
1/2 cup low-fat milk
1 1/2 teaspoons Worcestershire sauce
2 eggs

1/2 teaspoon pepper
1 teaspoon salt
Canola oil for cooking
2 (12-ounce) bottles chili sauce
2 (12-ounce) jars Concord grape jam or
  grape jelly

Combine the ground sirloin, bread crumbs, onion, milk, Worcestershire sauce, eggs, pepper and salt in a bowl and mix well. Shape into small balls.

Coat the bottom of a heavy frying pan with canola oil and heat. Add a single layer of meatballs to the hot oil. Cook for 5 minutes or until cooked through and brown, turning frequently. Remove the meatballs and place on a platter covered with paper towels. Repeat with the remaining meatballs, adding additional oil as needed.

Combine the chili sauce and grape jam in a large saucepan and mix well. Heat over medium heat until the jelly melts, stirring occasionally. Add the meatballs. Simmer over medium-low heat for 30 minutes or until the meatballs are heated through.

Yield: 6 dozen meatballs

CRAB AND CHEESE TOAST SQUARES

2 cups shredded sharp Cheddar cheese
1/4 cup sliced green onions
1 (6-ounce) can lump crab meat

1 cup (about) mayonnaise
Pumpernickel or rye cocktail bread

Combine the cheese, green onions and crab meat in a bowl and mix well. Add enough mayonnaise to coat and bind the crab meat mixture and mix well. Spread over the bread slices and place on a baking sheet. Broil for 3 minutes or until the mixture bubbles and the cheese is browned.

KIDS FAVORITE: Omit the crab meat for an appetizer even your finicky four-year-old will love.

Yield: 4 to 5 dozen squares

LEMON DILL SALMON ROLL-UPS

3 ounces (or more) cream cheese,
    at room temperature
12 ounces smoked salmon
1 tablespoon chopped red onion
3/4 teaspoon dill weed

1 1/2 teaspoons capers, rinsed and drained
1 1/2 teaspoons grated lemon zest
3 large flour tortillas
Salt and pepper to taste

Layer the cream cheese, salmon, onion, dill weed, capers and lemon zest evenly over the tortillas. Season with salt and pepper.

Roll each tortilla up to enclose the filling, sealing with additional cream cheese if needed. Cut into 1/2-inch pieces. Arrange on a platter. Serve immediately or chill, covered, until ready to serve.

Yield: 12 servings

GOLDEN BAKED SHRIMP SHELLS

A perfect appetizer for cocktail parties with a surprising and beautiful presentation. During baking, the crescent rolls form a "seashell" around each individual shrimp.

1 (6-ounce) package cooked frozen shrimp, thawed, rinsed and drained, or 24 large cooked shrimp, rinsed and drained
1 garlic clove, minced
1 tablespoon minced fresh parsley

¼ teaspoon hot pepper sauce
1 tablespoon olive or vegetable oil
1 (8-ounce) can crescent rolls
2 tablespoons grated Parmesan cheese
Cocktail sauce

Stir-fry the shrimp, garlic, parsley and hot pepper sauce in olive oil in a medium skillet over medium-high heat for 1 minute. Remove from the heat.

Remove the rolls from the can; do not unroll. Cut each roll of dough into 12 slices. Place 1 inch apart on an ungreased baking sheet. Press half of each slice to flatten. Spoon about 1 teaspoon of the shrimp mixture on the flattened sides of the slices. Fold the dough over the shrimp mixture; do not seal. Sprinkle with the cheese. Bake at 375 degrees for 11 to 13 minutes or until golden brown. Serve warm with cocktail sauce.

Yield: 24 servings

HJWC MISSION STATEMENT—"Hinsdale Junior Woman's Club is a community service organization that strives to enrich our community, the lives of our members and their families. HJWC's mission is to offer members a network of resources and opportunities; and serve as a leader of volunteer and philanthropic service."

FIG TART WITH GOAT CHEESE AND PROSCIUTTO

An elegant and savory appetizer. Perfect with Champagne at a luncheon or cocktail party.

1 (7-ounce) sheet frozen puff pastry, thawed
1 (4- to 6-ounce) jar fig jam
4 ounces crumbled goat cheese
4 ounces thinly sliced prosciutto, torn into small pieces
1 green bell pepper, thinly sliced (optional)
Fresh thyme

Roll the pastry into a 7×15-inch rectangle on a lightly floured surface. Brush the outside 1/2-inch edge with water and fold over to create the tart shell. Place on a parchment-lined baking sheet. Bake at 375 degrees for 25 to 30 minutes. Layer the jam, cheese, prosciutto and bell pepper in the shell. Bake for an additional 5 minutes. Sprinkle with thyme. Slice and serve.

Yield: 12 servings

SMOKED SALMON AND CAVIAR CREPE CAKE

Contributed by Paula Fuller Goss, this recipe is a favorite from The Second Floor's cooking school.

CREPES
3 tablespoons unsalted butter
1 cup all-purpose flour
3/4 cup cornstarch
Pinch of sugar
1/4 teaspoon salt
6 eggs
3 1/2 cups milk
3 tablespoons unsalted butter

CAKE
1 cup sour cream
2 tablespoons chopped fresh
   dill weed or chives
Finely grated zest of 1 lime
Salt
Freshly ground black pepper
1 1/4 pounds thinly sliced smoked salmon
3 1/2 ounces caviar

For the CREPES, melt 3 tablespoons butter in a small saucepan over medium heat. Swirl the pan until the butter turns a deep golden color. Remove from the heat and spoon off the clarified butter, discarding the solids. Let stand until cool. Whisk the flour, cornstarch, sugar and salt together in a bowl. Whisk in the clarified butter, eggs and milk. Pour into a pitcher. Chill, covered, for 1 to 12 hours. Line a baking sheet with parchment paper. Melt 3 tablespoons butter in a small saucepan over low heat. Heat an 8-inch nonstick skillet over medium heat. Stir the crepe batter gently. Brush a small amount of the melted butter over the bottom of the hot skillet. Lift the skillet up and pour 2 tablespoons of the batter into the skillet, tilting the pan to evenly cover the bottom. Cook until bubbles begin to appear on the surface and the underside is golden brown. Run a thin spatula around the edge of the crepe and turn the crepe. Cook for 20 seconds. Place on the prepared baking sheet. Repeat with the remaining batter.

For the CAKE, mix the sour cream, dill weed, lime zest, salt and pepper in a small bowl. Line a 6-inch round cake pan with plastic wrap. Alternate layers of crepes, the sour cream mixture and smoked salmon in the prepared pan until all ingredients are used. Wrap tightly and chill. You may freeze the cake for up to 2 weeks. Unwrap the cake and invert onto a serving plate. Spread the caviar over the top. Chill for 1 hour or longer. Cut into wedges and serve.

Yield: 6 to 8 servings

WITH ITS GREAT LOCATION, manicured lawns, and excellent schools, the western suburbs of Chicago are a popular place to settle and raise a family. Our neighborhoods are comprised of newly transplanted families who have moved to the Chicago area for their careers, as well as families that have lived here for generations. One of the oldest families in the area is the Fuller family. In 1843, Ben Fuller settled in the Brush Hill area near the intersection of present-day Ogden Avenue and York Road. One of the area's earliest settlers, Mr. Fuller petitioned the Chicago, Burlington, and Quincy Railroad to build a train line through the area. The Fuller family has grown considerably through the years, and many members of the family continue to live and work in the community. The Second Floor is one of several businesses, known for their impeccable service, owned and operated by the family.

SOUPS & Salads

This chapter has been generously sponsored by Turano Baking Company.

Photo: Curried Pumpkin Soup

CURRIED PUMPKIN SOUP

2 tablespoons butter
1 cup chopped onion
1 garlic clove, minced
1/2 teaspoon salt
1 teaspoon curry powder
1/4 teaspoon ground coriander

1/4 teaspoon ground white pepper
3 cups chicken broth
1 (15-ounce) can pumpkin
1 cup half-and-half
Sour cream (optional)
Chopped chives (optional)

Melt the butter in a large saucepan over medium-high heat. Add the onion. Sauté for 2 to 3 minutes or until tender. Add the garlic and cook for 1 minute. Add the salt, curry powder, coriander and white pepper. Cook for 1 minute. Stir in the broth and pumpkin. Bring to a boil. Reduce the heat to low. Cook for 15 to 20 minutes, stirring occasionally. Stir in the half-and-half. Cook for 5 minutes. Purée in batches in a food processor or blender. Serve warm. Garnish with sour cream and chives.

Yield: 6 servings

This recipe is pictured on page 39.

BUTTERNUT SQUASH SOUP

1 tablespoon butter or olive oil
1 onion, sliced
2 garlic cloves, chopped
3 carrots, sliced
2 celery ribs, sliced
1 potato, peeled and sliced

1 butternut squash, peeled, cut into
  2-inch cubes
5 1/4 cups chicken broth
1/3 cup honey
1/2 teaspoon dried thyme

Heat the butter in a large saucepan until melted. Add the onion and garlic. Cook for 3 to 5 minutes over medium heat, stirring occasionally. Stir in the carrots and celery. Cook for 5 minutes or until the celery is tender, stirring occasionally.

Add the potatoes, squash, broth, honey and thyme. Bring to a boil. Reduce the heat and simmer for 30 to 45 minutes or until the squash is tender. Let stand until cooled enough to purée. Purée in batches in a food processor or blender. Reheat and serve.

Yield: 6 servings

LIVING IN THE SUBURBS OF CHICAGO, we have access to all the city's rich cultural attractions, including its world-class museums, music, and theater. However, we do not have to travel downtown to enjoy fine theater and music. Formed in 1929, the Theater of Western Springs has been putting on theatrical productions and training aspiring actors for more than seventy years. In addition to offering music and art classes, the Hinsdale Center for the Arts sponsors chamber music concerts in local homes, featuring professional orchestral musicians. One can view the works of local artists at the LaGrange Art League. And on a hot summer night, you can head out to one of a number of local outdoor concerts and festivals.

CREAMY MUSHROOM, POTATO AND LEEK SOUP

3 tablespoons butter or margarine
3 leeks, white parts only, chopped
3 large carrots, sliced
6 cups chicken broth
1 tablespoon chopped dill weed
1 teaspoon salt
1/8 teaspoon pepper

1 bay leaf
2 pounds potatoes, peeled, chopped
  (about 5 potatoes)
1 pound mushrooms, sliced
2 tablespoons butter
1 cup half-and-half
1/4 cup all-purpose flour

Heat 3 tablespoons butter in a large saucepan until melted. Add the leeks and carrots. Cook for 5 minutes, stirring occasionally. Stir in the broth, dill weed, salt and pepper. Add the bay leaf and potatoes. Simmer, covered, for 15 minutes or until the potatoes are tender. Remove and discard the bay leaf. Sauté the mushrooms in 2 tablespoons butter in a separate pan. Whisk the half-and-half and flour together in a large cup until smooth. Stir into the soup. Stir the mushrooms into the soup. Cook just until thickened, stirring constantly.

Yield: 6 servings

FRENCH ONION SOUP

¼ cup (½ stick) butter
1 yellow onion, thinly sliced
2½ tablespoons all-purpose flour

6 cups beef broth
Dried or toasted slices of French bread
1½ cups shredded Gruyère cheese

Heat the butter in a large saucepan until it begins to foam. Add the onion. Cook until the onion begins to brown, stirring constantly. Sprinkle the flour over the onion and stir to combine. Bring the broth to a boil in a separate saucepan. Stir the broth into the onion mixture. Simmer for 10 minutes, stirring occasionally. Pour into 4 ovenproof bowls. Place the bread on top of the soup and sprinkle with the cheese. Broil until the cheese melts and is bubbly. Serve immediately.

Yield: 4 servings

ITALIAN SAUSAGE AND TORTELLINI SOUP

12 ounces Italian sausage
1 can French onion soup
1 soup can water
1 cup chopped cabbage

1 (14-ounce) can Italian-style
  stewed tomatoes
1 (7-ounce) package refrigerated
  cheese tortellini

Remove the sausage from the casing. Brown the sausage in a saucepan, stirring until crumbly; drain. Add the soup, water, cabbage, tomatoes and tortellini. Simmer for 30 minutes or until the tortellini is al dente. Serve with Parmesan cheese.

Yield: 6 servings

BLACK BEAN CHILI

Cinnamon and cumin give this a richer flavor than ordinary chili. Serve this the next time you invite friends over to watch the big game—they'll all ask for the recipe.

1 pound ground beef or turkey
1 1/2 cups finely chopped onions
2 garlic cloves, minced
1 tablespoon canola oil
1 (15-ounce) can diced tomatoes
1 (6-ounce) can tomato paste
1 (4-ounce) can diced green chiles
1 tablespoon chili powder

1 1/2 teaspoons cumin
1 1/2 teaspoons dried oregano
Pinch of cinnamon
1/2 cup water
1 (7-ounce) can corn
2 (15-ounce) cans black beans, drained
Sour cream to taste

Brown the ground beef in a skillet, stirring until crumbly; drain.

Cook the onions and garlic in hot canola oil in a large saucepan until tender. Add the cooked beef, tomatoes, tomato paste, green chiles, chili powder, cumin, oregano, cinnamon and water and stir to combine. Bring to a boil over medium heat. Reduce the heat and simmer for 10 minutes. Add the corn and beans. Cook until heated through, adding additional water to make of the desired consistency. Ladle into chili bowls and top with a dollop of sour cream.

Yield: 6 to 8 servings

PLATFORM TENNIS—One of the winter sports crazes in the Hinsdale area is platform tennis, or "paddle." Popular with men, women, and children alike, platform tennis is an outdoor racquet sport, similar to tennis. Hinsdale, with two courts at Burns Field and four courts at Katherine Legge Memorial Park, has one of the largest public paddle facilities in the country. Paddle players from the Hinsdale area, including a couple of nationally ranked teams, compete locally and nationally. In addition to being great exercise, paddle is a lot of fun!

WHITE CHILI

1 1/2 pounds boneless chicken breasts
2 onions, chopped
1 tablespoon olive oil
Salt and pepper to taste
4 garlic cloves, minced
7 ounces chopped mild green chiles
2 teaspoons cumin
1 1/2 teaspoons dried oregano
1/4 teaspoon ground cloves

1/4 teaspoon cayenne pepper
2 cans cannellini beans, drained
4 to 6 cups chicken stock or canned broth
3 cups shredded Monterey Jack cheese
   (about 12 ounces)
Sour cream
Salsa
Chopped fresh cilantro

Place the chicken in a large saucepan. Add enough cold water to cover. Bring to a simmer. Cook for 15 minutes or until the chicken is cooked through and tender; drain. Let stand until cool. Cut into pieces.

Sauté the onions in hot olive oil in a large saucepan for 10 minutes or until tender. Season with salt and pepper. Stir in the garlic, chiles, cumin, oregano, cloves and cayenne pepper. Sauté for 2 minutes. Add the beans. Pour in enough stock to make of the desired consistency. Stir to combine. Bring to a boil. Reduce the heat and simmer for 30 minutes or until the beans are very tender, stirring occasionally. Add the chicken and 1 cup of the cheese. Stir until the cheese is melted.

Ladle into chili bowls. Serve with the remaining cheese, sour cream, salsa and cilantro.

Yield: 8 servings

NEW ENGLAND CLAM CHOWDER

This "chowdah" has been passed down from a New England grandmother. It is delicious as an occasional break from counting fat grams.

8 potatoes, chopped
1/2 cup (1 stick) butter
1 cup chopped celery
1 cup chopped green bell pepper
1 cup chopped scallions
1/2 cup all-purpose flour
1 to 2 bottles clam juice
4 cups milk

2 cups half-and-half
2 1/2 tablespoons Worcestershire sauce
8 to 10 drops of Tabasco sauce
1 tablespoon salt
Generous dash of white pepper
4 (5- to 6-ounce) cans clams, drained
Chopped parsley

Place the potatoes in a large saucepan and cover with cold water. Bring to a boil. Reduce the heat and simmer until the potatoes are tender; drain.

Heat the butter in a large saucepan until melted. Add the celery, bell pepper and scallions. Cook until tender. Stir in the flour and cook for 2 minutes. Stir in the clam juice gradually, adding enough to make of the desired consistency. Stir in the milk and half-and-half. Bring to a boil, stirring constantly. Stir in the Worcestershire sauce, Tabasco sauce, salt and white pepper. Reduce the heat and simmer. Add the cooked potatoes and clams. Cook until heated through. Garnish with parsley. Serve warm with crackers.

Yield: 8 to 10 servings

SHRIMP GAZPACHO

3 ounces cream cheese
1 avocado
1 (1-quart) bottle clam and tomato juice
1/2 cup chopped peeled cucumber
1/3 cup thinly sliced green onions
2 tablespoons olive oil
2 tablespoons red wine vinegar

1 tablespoon sugar
1 teaspoon dill weed
1 garlic clove, crushed
Dash of lemon juice
8 ounces (50/60 count) shrimp, cooked
1/4 to 1/2 teaspoon Tabasco sauce
Salt and pepper to taste

Chop the cream cheese and avocado into bite-size pieces. Combine the cream cheese, avocado, juice, cucumber, green onions, olive oil, vinegar, sugar, dill weed, garlic and lemon juice in a large bowl. Stir in the shrimp. Season with the Tabasco sauce, salt and pepper. Refrigerate, covered, until chilled through. For enhanced flavor, chill for 1 day. You may add chopped zucchini or extra shrimp.

Yield: 4 to 6 servings

SALAD GREENS WITH CANDIED ALMONDS

1 cup almonds	2 teaspoons honey
2 tablespoons sugar	6 cups mesclun greens
1/2 teaspoon salt	1 Granny Smith apple, sliced
1/2 teaspoon black pepper	1 cup crumbled blue cheese
1/4 teaspoon cayenne pepper	1 cup raspberry vinaigrette salad dressing

Fill a small saucepan with water and bring the water to a boil. Add the almonds and cook for 20 seconds; drain. Toss the hot almonds with the sugar, salt, black pepper, cayenne pepper and honey in a bowl. Spread over a parchment-lined baking sheet. Bake at 350 degrees for 25 to 30 minutes, stirring once. Let stand for 15 minutes or longer. You may store the almonds in an airtight container for up to 2 weeks; do not refrigerate.

Place the greens in a large salad bowl. Add the apple, blue cheese, candied almonds and salad dressing and toss. Serve immediately.

Yield: 6 servings

RED LEAF SALAD

2 tablespoons honey
2 tablespoons red wine vinegar
2 tablespoons Dijon mustard
1/2 cup olive oil

2 heads red leaf lettuce
1 large red onion, thinly sliced
1 (11-ounce) can mandarin oranges, drained

Combine the honey, vinegar and Dijon mustard in a bowl. Add the olive oil in a fine stream, whisking constantly. Tear the lettuce into bite-size pieces and place in a salad bowl. Add the onion and toss. Add the dressing and toss to coat. Garnish with mandarin oranges. Serve immediately.

Yield: 6 to 8 servings

SWEET SPINACH AND STRAWBERRY POPPY SEED SALAD

SESAME SEED DRESSING
2 tablespoons sesame seeds
1 tablespoon poppy seeds
1/2 cup sugar
1 1/2 teaspoons minced onion
1 1/4 teaspoons Worcestershire sauce
1/4 teaspoon paprika
1/4 cup cider vinegar
1/2 cup canola or vegetable oil

SALAD
2 bags of prewashed salad spinach, stemmed
1 pint strawberries, hulled and sliced

For the **DRESSING**, combine the sesame seeds, poppy seeds, sugar, onion, Worcestershire sauce and paprika in a bowl and mix well. Stir in the vinegar. Add the oil in a fine stream, whisking constantly.

For the **SALAD**, toss the spinach, strawberries and dressing together in a salad bowl. Serve immediately.

Yield: 6 servings

WARM SPINACH SALAD

DRESSING
¼ cup sugar
¼ cup white vinegar
¼ teaspoon salt
¼ teaspoon dry mustard
¼ teaspoon instant minced onion
Dash of paprika
1 egg yolk, lightly beaten
¼ cup vegetable oil

SALAD
5 cups torn fresh spinach
5 cups torn romaine
1 (11-ounce) can mandarin oranges, drained
1 red onion, thinly sliced, separated
    into rings
⅓ cup toasted walnuts

For the **DRESSING**, combine the sugar, vinegar, salt, mustard, onion, paprika and egg yolk in a small saucepan and mix well. Bring to a boil and boil for 1 minute. Stir in the oil gradually. Let stand until room temperature.

For the **SALAD**, combine the spinach, romaine, mandarin oranges, onion and walnuts in a salad bowl. Add the dressing and toss to combine. Serve immediately.

NOTE: Be careful when you toast the walnuts—they burn easily!

Yield: 8 servings

WE ARE GIVEN the ingredients of happiness, but the mixing is left to ourselves.

—Ethel M. Dell

WARM GOAT CHEESE SALAD

GOAT CHEESE
1 (10-ounce) log goat cheese
1/4 cup extra-virgin olive oil
1 tablespoon fresh thyme
1 cup fine bread crumbs
1 teaspoon dried thyme
Salt and pepper to taste

VINAIGRETTE
1 tablespoon balsamic vinegar
2 tablespoons freshly squeezed orange juice
Salt and pepper to taste
1 teaspoon dried thyme
1/2 cup olive oil
3 bunches arugula
1 teaspoon grated orange zest

For the GOAT CHEESE, cut the cheese into twelve rounds. Arrange in a single layer in a shallow dish. Pour the olive oil over the cheese. Sprinkle with the fresh thyme. Marinate in the refrigerator, covered, for 12 hours or longer; drain. Combine the bread crumbs, dried thyme, salt and pepper in a small bowl. Dredge each cheese round in the crumb mixture to coat and place on a baking sheet. Bake at 375 degrees for 8 minutes or until golden.

For the VINAIGRETTE, whisk the vinegar, orange juice, salt, pepper and thyme together in a bowl. Add the olive oil gradually, whisking constantly.

To assemble, toss the arugula with the vinaigrette in a large bowl. Arrange evenly over six plates. Place two goat cheese rounds over the greens on each plate. Sprinkle with the orange zest. Serve immediately.

Yield: 6 servings

CRANBERRY WALDORF SALAD

Coarsely chopped apples, cranberries, and nuts served on individual romaine lettuce leaves. This makes a beautiful first course for your next dinner party.

1 1/2 cups fresh or frozen cranberries
1/4 cup sugar
1 teaspoon grated orange zest
2 large Granny Smith apples,
   coarsely chopped
1 cup chopped walnuts
1/4 cup sliced green onions

1/2 cup golden raisins
2 tablespoons freshly squeezed lime juice
2 teaspoons Dijon mustard
2 teaspoons sugar
1/2 cup vegetable or olive oil
1 head romaine

Coarsely chop the cranberries. Combine with 1/4 cup sugar and orange zest in a bowl. Chill, covered, for 12 hours.

Combine the apples, walnuts, onions, raisins and cranberry mixture in a bowl. Combine the lime juice, Dijon mustard and 2 teaspoons sugar in a blender container. Add the oil gradually, processing until the mixture is smooth. Pour over the cranberry mixture and mix well. Chill, covered, for 1 to 4 hours.

Line a large platter with romaine leaves. Spoon the cranberry salad over the romaine.

Yield: 8 servings

LIFE IS *Delicious*

GREEN PEPPER, GREEN OLIVE AND TOMATO SALAD

Recipe contributed by Nancee Biank, Director of Children and Family Services at Wellness House.

3 green bell peppers, chopped
2 large tomatoes, chopped
1 Vidalia or sweet onion, chopped
1 cup stuffed green olives
1/2 cup chopped celery
1 (14-ounce) can artichoke hearts, drained, quartered (optional)

1 tablespoon oregano (optional)
1 teaspoon salt
1/4 teaspoon black pepper
1/4 cup olive oil
1/4 cup wine vinegar

Combine the bell peppers, tomatoes, onion, olives, celery, artichoke hearts, oregano, salt and pepper in a bowl and mix well. Whisk the olive oil and vinegar together in a separate bowl. Pour over the salad and toss to combine. Refrigerate, covered, until chilled through. You may increase the dressing by combining equal portions of olive oil and wine vinegar.

Yield: 6 servings

THE FAMILY MATTERS PROGRAM at the Wellness House, a program devoted to counseling children when cancer has stricken the family, was the HJWC's primary philanthropy during the club years 2004–2005 and 2005–2006. In addition to raising over $400,000 for the program, club members completed many hands-on service projects, including the creation of *The Family Matters Cookbook.*

"Creating lasting memories through a cookbook is so much fun! You are not only sharing recipes, but combining cultures and customs from so many people that a unique tapestry is formed. As the Director of Children and Family Services at Wellness House last year, I had the wonderful opportunity to work with the Hinsdale Junior Woman's Club and be a part of the tapestry that was created there. The enthusiasm, the laughter, and the passion that was exhibited throughout the two years we worked together all comes flooding back. Thank you again, Hinsdale Junior Woman's Club, for making families matter at Wellness House and everywhere you put your efforts!"

—*Nancee Biank*

ITALIAN CHOPPED SALAD

SHERRY-SHALLOT VINAIGRETTE

2 tablespoons sherry wine vinegar
1 tablespoon minced shallots
1 tablespoon Dijon mustard
1/4 cup olive oil
Salt and pepper to taste

SALAD

5 plum tomatoes, chopped
2 small heads Belgian endive, chopped
1 (8-ounce) package fresh mozzarella balls,
    cut into 1/2-inch pieces
2 cups chopped arugula (about 3 ounces)
1 cup chopped radicchio (about 1/4 head)
Salt and pepper to taste

For the VINAIGRETTE, whisk the vinegar, shallots and Dijon mustard together in a small bowl. Whisk in the olive oil gradually. Season with salt and pepper.

For the SALAD, combine the tomatoes, endive, mozzarella, arugula, and radicchio together in a salad bowl. Toss with enough vinaigrette to coat. Season with salt and pepper.

Yield: 4 first course or 2 main course servings

SWEET BASIL AND TOMATO CORN SALAD

This colorful salad has been a big hit at many summer barbecues.

6 ears corn, shucked
1/2 cup chopped orange bell pepper
1/2 cup chopped shallots
1/2 cup chopped cherry tomatoes
3 tablespoons apple cider vinegar

3 tablespoons olive oil
1/2 teaspoon kosher salt
1/2 teaspoon freshly ground pepper
1/2 cup thinly sliced fresh basil leaves

Bring enough water to cover the corn to a boil in a large saucepan. Add the corn and cook for 3 minutes. Drain and rinse with cold water. Cut the kernels off the cob when the corn is cool enough to handle. Combine the bell pepper, corn, shallots, tomatoes, vinegar, olive oil, salt and pepper in a large bowl and mix well. Stir in the basil just before serving.

Yield: 6 to 8 servings

BLOCK PARTIES—The block party is a favorite end-of-summer tradition in our towns. On Saturday afternoons in the late summer there are scores of streets closed to traffic. Neighbors gather to grill in the streets and enjoy each other's company. On occasion one of the village's fire engines will come to show off its sirens for the kids. Moon jumps, water balloon tosses, and scavenger hunts are always lots of fun. In Western Springs, one block has a legendary egg toss with a trophy that is proudly displayed on the winner's mantel until the following year's party. Whatever the entertainment, there is always great food and a good time had by all!

ASIAGO TORTELLINI SALAD

DRESSING
2 teaspoons lemon pepper
1/4 cup tarragon vinegar
1/2 cup red wine vinegar
Juice of 1 lemon
Salt to taste
1 cup olive oil

SALAD
1 red onion, chopped
1 bunch green onions, chopped
8 ounces deli prosciutto, chopped
2 (14-ounce) cans marinated artichoke
    hearts, drained and quartered
1 cup grated asiago cheese
1 pound cheese tortellini, fresh or frozen

For the **DRESSING**, combine the lemon pepper, vinegars, lemon juice and salt in a bowl and mix well. Add the olive oil in a fine stream, whisking constantly. Chill for 12 hours or longer.

For the **SALAD**, combine the red onion, green onions, prosciutto, artichoke hearts and cheese in a bowl and mix well. Cook the tortellini according to the package directions; drain. Rinse with cold water to chill. Add to the onion mixture and toss to combine. Add the dressing 1 hour before serving and toss to combine.

Yield: 8 servings

POTATO SALAD

This is not your everyday potato salad. Yogurt and sour cream provide a fresh twist on a backyard barbecue classic.

3 1/2 pounds small red potatoes
Salt
6 3/4 teaspoons red wine vinegar
3 3/4 teaspoons vegetable oil
3 3/4 teaspoons Dijon mustard
3/4 teaspoon finely chopped fresh basil
1/4 teaspoon pepper
1/2 teaspoon salt or to taste

2/3 cup plain yogurt
1/3 cup sour cream
1 teaspoon minced garlic
3/4 cup finely chopped red onion
3/4 cup chopped celery
5 bacon strips, crisp-cooked and crumbled
3 hard-cooked eggs, chopped

Combine the potatoes and a pinch of salt with enough water to cover in a large saucepan. Bring to a boil. Cook until tender; drain. Let stand until cool enough to handle. Cut into bite-size pieces.

Combine the vinegar, oil, Dijon mustard, basil, pepper and 1/2 teaspoon salt in a large bowl and mix well. Add the warm potatoes and toss to coat. Let stand until the potatoes are completely cooled.

Combine the yogurt, sour cream and garlic in a separate bowl. Add the onion, celery, bacon and eggs and mix well. Add to the potato mixture and toss to combine. Chill for 3 hours or longer.

Yield: 8 to 10 servings

ANTIPASTO PASTA SALAD

2 tablespoons salt
1 tablespoon olive oil
1 pound rotini pasta
2 tablespoons minced garlic
1/2 teaspoon salt
3 tablespoons balsamic vinegar
1 teaspoon dried Italian herb mixture
1 teaspoon black pepper
1/4 teaspoon crushed red pepper

1/4 cup extra-virgin olive oil
1 1/2 cups 1/4-inch cubes provolone cheese
1 cup thinly sliced oil-packed sun-dried
   tomatoes, drained
1 cup thinly sliced salami (about 4 ounces)
1 cup thinly sliced prosciutto
   (about 4 ounces)
2 tablespoons chopped fresh basil

Bring 2 tablespoons salt, olive oil and 4 quarts water to a boil in a large pot over high heat. Add the rotini. Cook for 9 minutes or until al dente, stirring occasionally. Drain and rinse with cold running water until the pasta is cool.

Mash the garlic and 1/2 teaspoon salt together in a large bowl. Whisk in the vinegar, Italian herb mixture, black pepper and red pepper. Whisk in the olive oil gradually. Add the pasta, cheese, tomatoes, salami, prosciutto and basil. Toss to combine. Serve immediately or chill, covered, until ready to serve. The salad is best at room temperature.

Yield: 8 to 10 servings

LIFE IS *Delicious*

LEMON TARRAGON CHICKEN SALAD

Fresh lemon combined with tarragon makes this a delightful salad. Simply serve on a bed of fresh greens, or pile high on freshly baked croissants for a luncheon meal.

1 1/4 pounds boneless skinless
   chicken breasts
Salt
3/4 cup finely chopped celery
1/2 cup plus 3 tablespoons mayonnaise

1/4 cup finely chopped red onion
2 tablespoons fresh tarragon
2 tablespoons freshly squeezed lemon juice
1 teaspoon grated lemon zest
Salt and pepper to taste

Bring enough water to cover the chicken and a small amount of salt to a boil in a large pot. Add the chicken. Reduce the heat to medium-low. Simmer, covered, for 12 minutes or until the chicken is cooked through. Drain and let stand until cooled. Cut into 1/2-inch pieces.

Combine the celery, mayonnaise, onion, tarragon, lemon juice and lemon zest in a large bowl and mix well. Add the chicken and mix well. Season with salt and pepper. Chill, covered, for up to 4 hours.

Yield: 6 servings

ORANGE CASHEW CHOPPED CHICKEN SALAD

Orange juice and red wine vinegar make this a light, healthy, and refreshing summertime favorite.
It tastes great and looks beautiful.

DRESSING
1/2 cup Italian flat-leaf parsley
1/4 cup orange juice
1 1/2 teaspoons red wine vinegar
1 1/2 teaspoons Dijon mustard
1 teaspoon salt
2 teaspoons sugar
1/4 cup olive oil

SALAD
2 (14-ounce) cans chicken broth
1 1/2 pounds boneless skinless chicken breasts
1/2 cup sliced celery
1/2 cup orange bell pepper, chopped
1/2 cup red bell pepper, chopped
1/4 cup sliced green onions
1/2 head romaine
1 cup cashews, halved
1 (4-ounce) can mandarin oranges

For the **DRESSING**, whisk the parsley, orange juice, vinegar, Dijon mustard, salt and sugar together in a bowl. Whisk in the olive oil gradually.

For the **SALAD**, bring the broth to a boil in a large skillet. Add the chicken. Cook, covered, for 15 minutes. Reduce the heat to low. Cook for 15 minutes or until the chicken is cooked through; drain. Let stand until cool. Cut into bite-size pieces. Combine the chicken, celery, bell peppers and green onions in a bowl and toss to combine. Add the dressing and toss to coat. Arrange the romaine on a platter. Spoon the salad over the romaine. Garnish with cashews and oranges.

Yield: 6 servings

ORIENTAL CHICKEN SALAD

SALAD
1 1/2 pounds boneless chicken breasts
Teriyaki sauce of choice
8 ounces slivered almonds
8 ounces salted sunflower seeds
1 bunch green onions, chopped
1 (16-ounce) package broccoli slaw
2 packages uncooked oriental ramen
   noodles, crushed

DRESSING
1/2 cup sugar
1/3 cup canola or vegetable oil
1/3 cup cider vinegar
1/4 cup water
2 flavor packets from oriental ramen noodles

For the SALAD, arrange the chicken in a single layer in a shallow nonreactive dish. Pour the teriyaki sauce over the chicken. Marinate, covered, in the refrigerator for 12 hours or longer; drain. Place the chicken in a baking dish. Bake at 375 degrees for 30 minutes. Cut into bite-size pieces. Combine the chicken, almonds, sunflower seeds, green onions and slaw in a bowl and toss to combine.

For the DRESSING, combine the sugar, canola oil, vinegar, water and contents of the flavoring packets in a bowl and mix well.

Add the noodles and dressing to the chicken salad and toss to combine. Serve immediately.

Yield: 6 servings

Entrées

Photo: Cranberry- and Apple-Stuffed Chicken Breasts with Raspberry Balsamic Drizzle

CRANBERRY- AND APPLE-STUFFED CHICKEN BREASTS WITH RASPBERRY BALSAMIC DRIZZLE

CHICKEN
6 (4-ounce) boneless skin-on chicken breasts
1 1/2 cups olive oil
3/4 cup white wine
Juice of 2 lemons
1 tablespoon chopped garlic
1/2 cup chopped onion
1 tablespoon kosher salt
1 1/2 teaspoons freshly ground black pepper
1/3 cup flat-leaf parsley

STUFFING
1/2 cup chopped onion
1/2 cup chopped celery
3/4 cup peeled chopped Granny Smith apple
3/4 cup (1 1/2 sticks) melted butter
1 1/2 teaspoons rubbed sage
3/4 cup dried cranberries
1/2 teaspoon kosher salt
1/4 teaspoon freshly ground black pepper
2 1/4 cups chicken stock
1 (14-ounce) package herb stuffing mix

RASPBERRY BALSAMIC DRIZZLE
1 cup balsamic vinegar
1/2 cup seedless raspberry preserves
Sage for garnish

For the **CHICKEN**, arrange the chicken in a single layer in a shallow dish. Combine the olive oil, wine, lemon juice, garlic, onion, salt, pepper and parsley in a bowl and mix well. Pour over the chicken. Chill, covered, for 12 hours or longer.

For the **STUFFING**, sauté the onion, celery and apple in the butter in a saucepan until tender. Stir in the sage, cranberries, salt, pepper and stock. Bring to a boil. Add the stuffing mix and mix well. Drain the chicken, discarding the marinade. Stuff each chicken breast generously between the skin and the meat with the stuffing. Arrange the stuffed chicken in a baking dish. Spoon any remaining stuffing around the chicken. Bake at 375 degrees for 1 hour, covering for the last 15 minutes if necessary. Arrange on a platter.

For the **DRIZZLE**, pour the vinegar in a small saucepan. Cook over low heat for 8 to 10 minutes or until the vinegar is thick and syrupy and reduced to 2 tablespoons; do not boil. Stir in the preserves. Drizzle over the chicken. Garnish with sage.

Yield: 6 servings

This recipe is pictured on page 63.

CHICKEN IN LEMON CREAM SAUCE

Excellent served over a bed of angel hair pasta and sautéed spinach.

1/4 cup (1/2 stick) butter or margarine
8 boneless skinless chicken breasts
2 tablespoons white wine
1/2 teaspoon grated lemon zest
2 tablespoons lemon juice
1/4 teaspoon salt

1/8 teaspoon white pepper
1 cup heavy cream
1/3 cup grated Parmesan cheese
1 cup sliced mushrooms
Red grapes
Lemon peel

Heat the butter in a large skillet over medium heat until melted. Add the chicken. Cook for 10 minutes or until the chicken is brown and tender, turning once. Place the chicken in an ovenproof serving dish. Discard the butter from the skillet. Combine the wine, lemon zest and lemon juice in the skillet. Cook for 1 minute over medium heat, stirring constantly. Stir in the salt and pepper. Pour in the cream gradually, stirring constantly. Cook until hot, stirring constantly; do not boil. Pour over the chicken. Sprinkle the chicken with the cheese and mushrooms. Broil 6 inches from the heat source until light brown. Garnish with grapes and lemon peel.

Yield: 8 servings

HONEY-MARINATED GRILLED CHICKEN

2 pounds chicken pieces	2 tablespoons crushed garlic
1 cup soy sauce	1/2 cup lemon juice
1 cup olive oil	1/2 cup white wine
1/2 cup honey	

Arrange the chicken in a single layer in a shallow dish. Combine the soy sauce, olive oil, honey, garlic, lemon juice and wine in a bowl and mix well. Pour over the chicken, turning to coat the chicken. Marinate, covered, in the refrigerator for 5 to 6 hours; drain.

Place the chicken skin side down on a grill rack over the fire. Grill for 10 minutes or until the skin is crisp, moving the chicken as needed to prevent charring. Move the chicken opposite the fire and grill skin side up. Grill for 15 minutes or until the chicken is cooked through.

Yield: 4 to 6 servings

PRIMARY PHILANTHROPY: "Building Partnerships in Unity"—Every two years, the HJWC active members select an organization as our primary philanthropy. The chosen organization receives our support through volunteer services and charitable donations. The selection process is always heart-wrenching since there are so many wonderful organizations in need of support. For the 2006–2008 club years, HJWC selected The Center for Independence in Countryside, Illinois. The mission of the Center is to help children with profound physical disabilities, such as cerebral palsy, gain physical independence through Conductive Education.

PESTO GOAT CHEESE CHICKEN

2 pounds boneless skinless chicken breasts
(about 4 large chicken breasts)
4 ounces pesto
4 ounces goat cheese

Salt and pepper to taste
1 cup all-purpose flour
2 tablespoons olive oil

Pound the chicken into 1/2-inch thickness between sheets of waxed paper. Spread 1 ounce pesto on each piece of chicken. Crumble 1 ounce goat cheese over the pesto on each piece of chicken. Fold each chicken breast in half to enclose the filling and secure with a wooden pick. You may roll the chicken, beginning with the short side, to enclose the filling. Season with salt and pepper. Dredge in flour to coat. Heat the olive oil in an ovenproof skillet until hot. Add the chicken and cook until brown on all sides. Place in a 350-degree oven. Bake for 25 minutes or until the chicken is cooked through.

Yield: 4 to 6 servings

CAJUN CHICKEN PASTA

1 pound angel hair pasta
1/2 cup (1 stick) butter
1 to 2 tablespoons Creole seasoning
1 pound boneless skinless chicken breasts,
cut into 1/2-inch strips
3 cups sliced mushrooms (optional)

1 teaspoon minced garlic
1/4 cup minced green onions
3 tablespoons chopped parsley
1 cup chicken broth
1/4 cup (1/2 stick) butter

Cook the pasta according to the package directions; drain.

Heat 1/2 cup butter in a large skillet until melted. Add the seasoning. Add the chicken and cook for 2 minutes or until brown, stirring occasionally. Stir in the mushrooms and cook for 2 minutes. Stir in the garlic and cook for 2 minutes. Add the green onions, parsley and broth. Cook for 2 minutes or until rapidly boiling. Add 1/4 cup butter. Cook for 5 minutes, continuing to boil.

Place the pasta in a serving bowl. Spoon the chicken and sauce over the pasta.

Yield: 4 to 6 servings

PASTA WITH CHICKEN, ARTICHOKE HEARTS AND ROASTED RED PEPPER

This is a warm, comforting dish to bring to a neighbor with a new baby or a friend feeling under the weather.

8 ounces tri-color fusilli
3 tablespoons olive oil
12 ounces boneless skinless chicken breasts
1 large onion, sliced
2 garlic cloves, minced

2 (6-ounce) jars marinated artichoke hearts
1 (7-ounce) jar roasted red peppers,
   sliced if needed
1/2 cup pitted black olives (optional)
Grated Parmesan cheese to taste

Cook the pasta according to the pasta directions; drain.

Heat the olive oil in a skillet. Add the chicken and cook until browned on both sides. Reduce the heat. Cover and cook for 10 minutes or until cooked through. Cut into strips. Set aside and keep warm. Add the onion to the pan drippings. Cook until almost tender. Add the garlic and cook until the onion is tender. Add the artichoke hearts, red peppers, olives and chicken. Cook until heated through. Pour over the pasta and mix well. Sprinkle with cheese. You may prepare the sauce ahead of time and chill, covered, in the refrigerator.

Yield: 2 to 3 servings

ARROZ CON POLLO

It's comfort food Latin style. This classic Cuban dish is sure to warm your belly and your soul.

10 chicken pieces (about 2 whole chickens)
2 tablespoons vegetable oil
1/4 cup olive oil
3 large onions, chopped
6 large garlic cloves, chopped
1 green bell pepper, chopped
1 (8-ounce) can unseasoned tomato sauce
1/2 teaspoon cumin
2 bay leaves

2 chicken bouillon cubes
1 cup boiling water
3 bottles beer (about 4 1/2 cups)
1 (8-ounce) jar pimentos
3 cups Valencia or long grain white rice
1 1/2 tablespoons salt
1 teaspoon Bijol or saffron
2 cups water
2 cups sweet peas

Sauté the chicken in hot vegetable oil in a skillet over medium heat until brown on all sides. Heat the olive oil in a large pot. Add the onions, garlic and bell pepper. Sauté over low heat for 10 to 15 minutes or until tender. Add the tomato sauce, cumin and bay leaves. Cook for 3 to 4 minutes. Remove and discard the bay leaves. Add the chicken, spooning the sauce over the chicken to cover. Dissolve the bouillon cubes in the boiling water in a measuring cup. Pour over the chicken. Pour 1 bottle of beer over the chicken. Cover and bring to a boil. Boil for 15 minutes. Drain the pimentos, reserving the juice. Add the reserved juice, remaining 2 bottles beer, rice, salt, Bijol and 2 cups water to the chicken. Reduce the heat. Simmer, covered, for 40 minutes or until the rice is very soft.

Bring enough water to cover the peas to a boil in a saucepan. Add the peas. Cook for 8 minutes or until heated; drain.

Spoon the arroz con pollo into a large serving bowl. Garnish with the pimentos and peas.

Yield: 10 to 12 servings

CRISPY OVEN CHICKEN FINGERS

These are great for a family dinner. The kids will love them. For a fun party idea, serve them as an appetizer with a smorgasbord of your favorite dipping sauces.

2 pounds boneless skinless chicken breasts, cut into 3x1/2-inch strips
2 cups buttermilk
2 garlic cloves, crushed
1 tablespoon hot pepper sauce
1 teaspoon kosher salt

1 teaspoon freshly ground pepper
Olive oil
1 (7-ounce) package sesame crispbread or sesame crackers, crushed
6 tablespoons (3/4 stick) butter, melted

Arrange the chicken in a shallow dish. Combine the buttermilk, garlic, hot pepper sauce, salt and pepper in a bowl and mix well. Pour over the chicken. Marinate, covered, in the refrigerator for 2 to 12 hours; drain.

Brush 2 baking pans with olive oil. Combine the crushed crackers and butter in a bowl and mix well. Dredge the chicken in the cracker mixture to coat and place in the prepared pans. Bake at 400 degrees for 25 minutes or until golden and crisp, turning once. These are excellent with dipping sauce.

KIDS' FAVORITE: Omit the hot pepper sauce for kids' chicken fingers.

Yield: About 32 pieces

SESAME BAKED CHICKEN

3 1/2 pounds chicken pieces
3 tablespoons soy sauce
1 1/2 teaspoons minced fresh ginger

1/2 cup sesame oil
1/4 teaspoon crushed red pepper
1/2 cup sesame seeds

Arrange the chicken pieces in a shallow baking dish. Combine the soy sauce, ginger, sesame oil and red pepper in a bowl and mix well. Pour over the chicken. Marinate in the refrigerator for 90 minutes. Sprinkle with the sesame seeds. Bake at 400 degrees for 25 to 35 minutes or until the chicken is cooked through.

Yield: 6 servings

TURKEY LASAGNA WITH GOAT CHEESE AND BASIL

This is a more sophisticated lasagna that you'll want to make over and over again.

1 tablespoon olive oil
1 tablespoon butter
1 cup chopped onion
1 garlic clove, chopped
1/4 teaspoon freshly grated nutmeg
1 1/2 pounds ground turkey
1 (28-ounce) can crushed tomatoes in
   tomato purée
1 (6-ounce) can tomato paste
1/4 cup chopped fresh flat-leaf parsley

1/2 cup chopped fresh basil leaves
2 teaspoons kosher salt
1 teaspoon freshly ground black pepper
8 ounces lasagna noodles
15 ounces ricotta cheese
4 ounces goat cheese, crumbled
1 1/4 cups grated Parmesan cheese
1 egg, lightly beaten
1 pound fresh mozzarella cheese, thinly sliced
Fresh basil for garnish

Heat the olive oil and butter in a large skillet over medium heat. Add the onion. Cook for 3 to 4 minutes or until tender. Add the garlic and nutmeg and cook for 1 minute. Add the turkey. Cook over medium-low heat for 8 to 10 minutes or until brown and crumbly, stirring frequently. Stir in the tomatoes, tomato paste, 2 tablespoons of the parsley, basil, 1 1/2 teaspoons of the salt and 1/2 teaspoon of the pepper. Bring to a simmer. Cook for 15 to 20 minutes or until thickened.

Place the noodles in a bowl and cover with very hot water. Let stand for 20 minutes; drain.

Combine the ricotta cheese, goat cheese, 1 cup of the Parmesan cheese, egg, remaining 2 tablespoons parsley, remaining 1/2 teaspoon salt, and remaining 1/2 teaspoon pepper in a bowl and mix well.

Spread 1/3 of the sauce evenly over the bottom of a 9×12-inch baking dish. Layer the pasta, mozzarella cheese, ricotta mixture and remaining sauce one-half at a time over the sauce. Sprinkle with the remaining 1/4 cup Parmesan cheese. Bake at 400 degrees for 30 minutes or until hot and bubbly. Garnish with fresh basil.

Yield: 8 servings

PENNE PASTA WITH ITALIAN TURKEY SAUSAGE AND BROCCOLI

1 red bell pepper
1 yellow bell pepper
1 pound penne pasta
1 pound turkey Italian sausage
2 or 3 garlic cloves, minced
1 (28-ounce) can Italian-seasoned tomatoes

Salt and pepper to taste
1 1/2 pounds broccoli, trimmed, cut into
  bite-size pieces
3/4 cup vegetable or chicken stock
1/4 cup olive oil
1 cup freshly grated Parmesan cheese

Place the bell peppers on a baking sheet. Roast the bell peppers on the top oven rack at 425 degrees for 20 minutes, turning frequently to blacken on all sides. Place in a dish and cover with plastic wrap. Let stand for 15 minutes. Run the peppers under cold water and remove the skin. Chop into bite-size pieces.

Bring a large pot of water to a boil. Add the pasta and cook until al dente or to desired degree of doneness; drain.

Brown the sausage in a skillet, stirring until crumbly; drain. Add the cooked peppers, garlic, tomatoes, salt and pepper. Cook for 3 minutes. Increase the heat to high. Add the broccoli and stock. Cook, covered, for 2 minutes or until the broccoli is bright green. Cook, uncovered, until the broccoli is tender-crisp. Toss with the pasta, olive oil and cheese in a large serving bowl.

Yield: 6 servings

GRAND MARNIER ROAST DUCK

You don't have to go to a restaurant to enjoy roast duck. This is an easy dish to prepare even if you've never made duck.

GLAZE
1 cup orange marmalade
2 tablespoons distilled white vinegar
1/4 cup Grand Marnier
2 (4 1/2- to 5-pound) ducks or duck breasts

SAUCE
1 cup orange marmalade
1/4 cup distilled white vinegar
Pepper to taste
1 can whole cranberries
1/4 cup Grand Marnier
Whole cranberries
Orange slices

For the GLAZE, combine the marmalade and vinegar in a saucepan. Cook over medium heat until the marmalade melts, stirring occasionally. Strain into a separate saucepan, discarding the solids. Boil until reduced to 1/2 cup. Stir in the Grand Marnier.

Prick the skin several times on all sides of the ducks. Place breast side down on a rack in a roasting pan. Pour the glaze over the ducks. Roast at 350 degrees for 20 minutes. Turn the ducks over and baste with the glaze. Roast for 1 hour. Increase the temperature to 400 degrees and roast for 10 minutes or until the duck registers 180 degrees on a meat thermometer and is of the desired shade of brown. Place on a platter and let stand for 10 minutes.

For the SAUCE, combine the marmalade, vinegar and pepper. Bring to a boil, stirring occasionally. Add the cranberries. Reduce the heat and simmer for 15 minutes. Add the Grand Marnier.

Garnish the ducks and platter with whole cranberries and orange slices. Pour the glaze over the ducks. Serve any remaining glaze on the side with the ducks.

Yield: 6 to 8 servings

BEEF TENDERLOIN WITH SPICE RUB

1 tablespoon ground thyme
1 teaspoon white pepper
1 tablespoon seasoned salt
1 teaspoon garlic powder
¼ teaspoon oregano

1 (3- to 4-pound) trimmed beef tenderloin
1 teaspoon salt
¼ cup Worcestershire sauce
2 cups water

Combine the thyme, white pepper, seasoned salt, garlic powder and oregano in a bowl and mix well. Rub over the tenderloin. Wrap the tenderloin in foil and refrigerate for 12 hours or longer. Let stand at room temperature for 1 hour.

Place the tenderloin in a baking pan. Sprinkle with salt and Worcestershire sauce. Pour the water into the pan. Roast at 400 degrees for 45 minutes or to 140 degrees on a meat thermometer for medium-rare. Let the tenderloin stand for 10 minutes. Pour the pan juices into a separating cup and let stand. Pour the juices into a bowl and serve with the tenderloin.

Yield: 6 to 8 servings

BLUE CHEESE-STUFFED BEEF TENDERLOIN

This easy entrée will be sure to impress your friends and family. It is perfect for any celebration.

1 (3- to 4-pound) beef tenderloin
3/4 cup chopped pecans
1/4 cup chopped fresh parsley

Garlic powder to taste
3/4 cup crumbled blue cheese

Line a roasting pan with foil. Slice the tenderloin down the middle horizontally; do not cut through the back of the tenderloin. Place the tenderloin in the prepared pan and open it. Combine the pecans, parsley, garlic powder and cheese in a bowl and mix well. Spread the stuffing over the bottom half of the tenderloin. Fold the top over the stuffing and tie the tenderloin closed with butcher's twine. Roast at 400 degrees for 45 to 60 minutes or to 140 degrees on a meat thermometer for medium-rare. Slice the tenderloin and arrange on a platter, topping with any loose stuffing.

Yield: 6 to 8 servings

MARINATED SKIRT STEAK

This is a fabulous marinade that receives rave reviews—equally delicious on flank steak or your favorite cut of meat. You can even freeze a steak in the marinade for future barbecues and it will still be delicious.

1 cup orange juice
1/2 cup soy sauce
3 or 4 scallions, chopped
3 tablespoons brown sugar

2 tablespoons chopped peeled
  fresh ginger
2 garlic cloves, chopped
1 1/2 to 2 pounds skirt steak

Combine the orange juice, soy sauce, scallions, brown sugar, ginger and garlic in a sealable plastic bag and mix well. Add the skirt steak and seal the bag. Marinate in the refrigerator for 24 hours or longer; drain.

Grill the steak on high heat for 10 to 15 minutes or until the steak is of the desired degree of doneness, turning frequently to char the edges and caramelize the sugar. Slice and serve immediately.

Yield: 6 servings

BARBECUE BEEF SANDWICHES

1 (2½- to 3-pound) beef pot roast
½ cup (1 stick) butter
2 onions
1½ cups chopped celery
¼ cup vinegar
¼ cup sugar
4 teaspoons mustard

½ teaspoon black pepper
¼ teaspoon cayenne pepper
½ teaspoon salt
2 tablespoons lemon juice
1 cup ketchup
3 tablespoons Worcestershire sauce
8 to 10 buns

Place the roast in a large pot and cover with water. Bring to a boil. Boil for 1½ hours; drain. Shred the roast.

Heat the butter in a large pot until melted. Add the onions and celery and cook until tender, stirring occasionally. Add the vinegar, sugar, mustard, black pepper, cayenne pepper, salt and lemon juice. Simmer for 20 minutes. Add the shredded beef, ketchup and Worcestershire sauce. Simmer for 20 minutes. Serve on the buns.

Yield: 8 to 10 servings

OLD WORLD ITALIAN MEATBALLS AND SAUCE

This is an authentic Italian meatball and sauce recipe that has been handed down for generations. We invite you to make this part of your family traditions.

SAUCE

2 (28-ounce) cans Italian plum tomatoes
1 (6-ounce) can tomato paste
2 garlic cloves, minced
1 teaspoon dried basil
1 bay leaf
Salt and pepper to taste
1 pound Italian sausage
Vegetable oil

MEATBALLS

4 or 5 bread slices
1 pound ground round
1 garlic clove, minced
1/3 cup grated Romano cheese
1 tablespoon minced parsley
1/2 teaspoon salt
1/4 teaspoon pepper
4 eggs

For the SAUCE, purée the tomatoes in a blender until smooth. Pour into a large pot. Add the tomato paste, garlic, basil, bay leaf, salt and pepper and mix well. Bring to a boil over medium heat. Reduce the heat and simmer. Sauté the sausage in a small amount of oil in a skillet for 20 minutes or until cooked through. Cut into 2-inch pieces and stir into the sauce.

For the MEATBALLS, pulse the bread in a food processor until crumbly. Combine the ground round, garlic, cheese, parsley, salt and pepper in a bowl and mix well. Add the eggs and half the bread crumbs. Add additional crumbs until the mixture forms a ball. Shape into nine large meatballs with wet hands. Place the meatballs in a baking pan coated with oil. Bake at 350 degrees for 20 minutes or until cooked through; drain.

Add the meatballs to the sauce. Simmer, partially covered, for 1 hour, stirring frequently and being careful not to break the meatballs. Remove and discard the bay leaf.

Yield: 8 to 10 servings

"CHERISHED MEMORIES OF COOKING with Grandma Perry warm our heart every time we make this dish. Every child in the family, having reached a certain age, and every person marrying into the family was required at some point to spend a day in Grandma Perry's kitchen learning to cook. A pinch of this, a cup of that, she lovingly passed on the recipes that had been passed on to her."

STUFFED SHELLS

Delicious and easy, these stuffed pasta shells are perfect for weekday dinners with the family! This recipe was contributed by Eleanor and Mike Evangelides, founders of the Gus Foundation, which was HJWC's chosen primary philanthropy during the 2002–2004 club years.

2 packages large pasta shells
1 1/2 pounds ground beef
2 eggs
1 (12-ounce) package shredded
  mozzarella cheese

1/2 cup grated Parmesan cheese
3/4 package frozen chopped spinach,
  thawed, drained
1 jar Italian sauce

Cook the shells according to the package directions; drain. Brown the ground beef in a skillet, stirring until crumbly; drain. Whisk 2 eggs in a bowl. Add the hot browned beef and stir until the eggs are cooked. Stir in half the mozzarella, the Parmesan cheese and three-fourths of the spinach. Stuff each shell with the beef mixture and place in a large baking dish. Pour the sauce over the shells. Cover loosely with foil and poke holes in the foil to allow steam to escape. Bake at 350 degrees for 25 minutes. Sprinkle with the remaining mozzarella cheese. Bake for 5 to 10 minutes or until the cheese melts.

Yield: 8 servings

OVER THE YEARS, HJWC HAS HAD THE OPPORTUNITY TO WORK with a number of inspiring organizations that bring hope to those in need. The Gus Foundation is a not-for-profit organization established by the family and friends of Gus Evangelides, who died at twenty-one months old after a courageous battle with a malignant brain tumor. Committed to "providing hope for children with brain tumors," the Gus Foundation has worked tirelessly for the past eleven years raising funds for pediatric brain tumor research and family support programs. Their efforts culminated in the creation of the Gus Foundation Endowed Fellowship and the Gus Foundation Endowed Chair in Neuro-Oncology at Children's Memorial Hospital in Chicago. In addition to assisting with various hands-on service projects, HJWC was proud to help in this effort by raising more than $280,000 for pediatric brain tumor research during the 2002–2004 club years.

VEAL PICCATA

14 to 16 (¼-inch-thick) slices of veal cutlets
Salt and pepper
All-purpose flour
½ to ¾ cup (1 to 1½ sticks) butter
Juice of 2 lemons
3 to 4 tablespoons chopped parsley

Pound the veal between sheets of waxed paper to make as thin as possible. Sprinkle with salt and pepper. Coat with flour. Heat 5 to 6 tablespoons of butter in a skillet over high heat until golden. Add the veal in a single layer and cook for 2 minutes on each side or until browned. Place on a hot serving platter and keep warm. Repeat with the remaining veal, adding additional butter as needed. Add the lemon juice and parsley to the pan drippings. Gradually stir in any remaining butter. Pour over the veal.

Yield: 6 to 8 servings

GRILLED MINT BUTTERFLIED LAMB

1/2 cup soy sauce
6 garlic cloves, chopped
1 (6-pound) butterfly leg of lamb
1 (12-ounce) jar mint sauce
1/3 cup white wine

Rub the soy sauce and garlic over the lamb. Place in a sealable plastic bag. Pour the mint sauce and wine over the lamb and seal the bag. Marinate in the refrigerator for 24 hours; drain. Grill over hot coals for 30 minutes or to the desired degree of doneness.

Yield: 8 to 12 servings

MUSTARD HERB-CRUSTED PORK TENDERLOIN

2 (12- to 16-ounce) pork tenderloins
2 tablespoons Dijon mustard
1 cup Italian-style bread crumbs

Trim the tenderloins. Spread the Dijon mustard over the tenderloins and roll in the bread crumbs to coat. Place in a shallow baking dish. Bake at 350 degrees for 25 minutes or until cooked through.

Yield: 4 to 6 servings

JUNIOR CLOTHESLINE—One of the HJWC's long-standing partnerships is with Hinsdale Community Services (HCS). In an effort to develop a long-term volunteer opportunity for active and associate members, HJWC joined forces with HCS to help its clothing assistance program. During the 1997–1998 club year, HJWC members renovated a room in the Hinsdale Memorial Building—everything from new paint and carpeting to a closet organization system—and established "The Junior Clothesline." HJWC members hold clothing drives throughout the year and volunteer to assist HCS clients with finding clothes. Every Christmas, the HJWC sponsors "The Gift of Christmas," in which HCS clients are invited to "shop" at no cost for donated gifts for their children. The 2006 Gift of Christmas provided new books, hats, toys, socks, and games to 156 families benefitting a total of 551 children.

ROASTED ROSEMARY PORK LOIN

3 large garlic cloves, minced
4 teaspoons chopped fresh rosemary
1/2 teaspoon salt
1/2 teaspoon freshly ground pepper
3 tablespoons olive oil
2 tablespoons Dijon mustard
2 tablespoons freshly squeezed lemon juice
1 (5-pound) center-cut pork loin roast

Preheat the oven to 400 degrees. Combine the garlic, rosemary, salt, pepper, olive oil, Dijon mustard and lemon juice in a bowl and mix well. Spread over the fat side of the roast. Place fat side up on a rack in a roasting pan. Reduce the oven temperature to 325 degrees. Roast for 2 hours.

Yield: 4 to 6 servings

SENATORE RENATO TURANO STUFFED PORK CHOPS

This delicious stuffed pork chop recipe comes from Senatore Renato Turano and his family. Turano artisan bread, Italian sausage, Gorgonzola cheese, and sun-dried tomatoes create a savory stuffing, rich with authentic Italian taste. The stuffing is also fabulous with chicken. Buon appetito!

12 ounces Italian sausage
2 garlic cloves, minced
2 tablespoons oil from sun-dried tomatoes or olive oil
2 tablespoons sun-dried tomatoes, chopped

¼ cup pine nuts
2 cups crumbled fresh Turano Italian bread
¼ cup white wine
4 ounces crumbled Gorgonzola cheese
4 to 6 center-cut pork chops

Remove the sausage from the casing. Brown the sausage in a skillet, stirring until crumbly; drain. Sauté the garlic in the oil in a separate skillet. Add the cooked sausage and cook until browned and crisp, stirring frequently. Stir in the sun-dried tomatoes, pine nuts and bread. Cook until the nuts begin to change color, stirring frequently. Add the wine and cook until almost all of the liquid is evaporated. Stir in the cheese. Remove from the heat.

Cut a pocket in each pork chop and fill with the stuffing. Close the pockets with wooden picks. Place the stuffed pork chops in a baking dish. Sprinkle with any remaining stuffing. Bake at 350 degrees for 35 to 45 minutes or until cooked through.

Yield: 4 to 6 servings

ETHNIC HERITAGE, reflected in our foods, is a source of great pride in our neighborhoods and in our hearts. Families pass down recipes and stories from "the old country," and parents strive to teach their children the language and culture of their ancestors. Renato Turano is a proud, successful Italian American businessman who has dedicated his life to sharing that success. Born in Calabria, Italy, Turano moved to Chicago in the late 1950s with his brothers and parents to pursue the American dream. The family bought a small company in 1962 and transformed it into one of the largest manufacturers of artisan breads in the country, the Turano Baking Company. Throughout his life, Turano has been active in supporting the Italian American community. With dual U.S. and Italian citizenship, in 2006 Turano was an elected Senator to the Italian Republic, representing the interests of Italian citizens living abroad.

ROB JOHNSON'S JAMBALAYA

This spicy jambalaya is delicious served with corn bread or a crusty baguette.

4 bay leaves	1 (1-pound) Polish sausage
1 teaspoon salt	1 1/2 cups chopped onions
1 teaspoon white pepper, or to taste	1 1/2 cups chopped celery
1 teaspoon cayenne pepper, or to taste	1 cup chopped green bell pepper
1/2 teaspoon ground cumin	1/2 teaspoon minced garlic
1/2 teaspoon black pepper	2 cups rice
1/2 teaspoon dried thyme	4 cups water
1/4 cup (1/2 stick) butter	4 chicken bouillon cubes

Combine the bay leaves, salt, white pepper, cayenne pepper, cumin, black pepper and thyme in a small bowl and mix well. Set aside.

Melt the butter in an 8-quart pot over medium-high heat. Add the sausage. Cook for 5 minutes, stirring until crumbly. Stir in the seasoning mix, onions, celery, bell pepper and garlic. Cook for 10 to 12 minutes. Add the rice. Cook for 5 minutes, stirring constantly. Add the water and bouillon cubes. Bring to a boil. Reduce the heat. Simmer, covered, for 20 minutes or until the rice is tender. Remove and discard the bay leaves.

Yield: 6 servings

PRESENTLY A TELEVISION NEWS CO-ANCHOR at CBS 2-Chicago, Rob Johnson is a familiar face on Chicago television. A Hinsdale resident and HJWC spouse, Rob has graciously served as honorary emcee at several of our annual benefits. With his witty comments and charming personality, Rob has proven that he is as talented before a live audience as he is behind the news desk.

Rob's jambalaya recipe is unique because it uses Polish sausage rather than seafood, which gives the dish a completely different texture and personality. The recipe originated in Louisiana, where Rob's mother and grandmother both grew up.

Like most American children, Rob grew up on burgers and pizza, but if jambalaya was an option, it was his first choice. The warmth and spicy flavor was unforgettable, and two to three helpings was the norm.

Rob and his wife, Stacy, an HJWC member, host dinner parties in the winter, and jambalaya is often on the menu and enjoyed by guests as a hearty winter meal. Cut up some corn bread or French bread as a side and you will have some happy eaters!

The HJWC is grateful to Rob Johnson for taking the time to help make our annual benefits a huge success.

TAGLIATELLE WITH PORCINI MUSHROOM PANCETTA SAUCE

Given to one of our members by Chef Luciano Benozzi at the Palazzo Bandino in Chianciano Terme, Italy, this is a rich pasta dish that comes straight from a Tuscany palazzo surrounded by sunflowers. Prepare this for your friends for an authentic taste of Italy in your own home.

½ cup extra-virgin olive oil
1 garlic clove, finely chopped
2 onions, finely chopped
3½ ounces pancetta, prosciutto or bacon, cut into small pieces
7 ounces porcini mushrooms, sliced
½ cup white wine

4 tomatoes, peeled, seeded, chopped or puréed
2 cups milk or cream
Salt
1 pound tagliatelle pasta
4 basil leaves, coarsely chopped

Heat the olive oil in a large pot. Add the garlic and onions. Cook until the onions are tender, stirring frequently. Stir in the pancetta. Add the mushrooms, wine and tomatoes. Cook for 4 to 10 minutes or until the sauce is of the desired consistency. Add the milk and bring to a simmer, stirring constantly. Simmer, stirring constantly.

Bring a large pot of water to a boil. Add a small amount of salt. Add the tagliatelle and cook until almost al dente; drain. Add to the sauce. Stir to combine; do not break the pasta. Stir in the basil. Serve immediately.

Yield: 6 servings

PEELING TOMATOES—To peel a tomato, first wash and detach the stem. Make a shallow *X* incision on the bottom of the tomato. Bring a pot of water to a boil and place the tomato in the boiling water. Remove the tomato after thirty seconds, or sooner if you see the skin begin to peel off. Then, submerge the tomato in a bowl of ice water and let stand for five minutes. Remove and peel the skin off with your hands, using a knife if necessary—just be sure not to squeeze the tomato.

REHYDRATING DRIED MUSHROOMS—It's much easier to find dried porcini mushrooms than fresh. Dried mushrooms offer an intense flavor and can be kept for years in a dry pantry. To rehydrate for use in recipes, soak the mushrooms in warm water for thirty minutes. Remove with a slotted spoon. The leftover liquid can be used to flavor soups and sauces.

GRILLED SALMON

1 (2-pound) salmon fillet
2 cups teriyaki sauce
½ cup (1 stick) butter
3 tablespoons lemon juice
1 tablespoon brown sugar

Place the salmon in a shallow dish. Pour the sauce over the salmon. Marinate for 1 hour; drain. Combine the butter, lemon juice and brown sugar in a bowl and mix well. Place salmon skin side down on a hot grill rack. Brush with the butter mixture. Grill for 5 minutes. Turn the salmon and brush with the butter mixture. Grill for 3 minutes. Turn the salmon and brush again with the butter mixture. Grill for 3 minutes.

Yield: 4 servings

HERB-GRILLED SALMON WITH TROPICAL SALSA

Set the stage for this tropical fare with drinks on the patio as the sun sets on a warm summer evening.

MANGO SALSA

1 cup chopped mango
1 cup sliced banana
1/4 cup chopped fresh mint
2 tablespoons freshly squeezed orange juice
1 teaspoon grated lime zest
1 tablespoon freshly squeezed lime juice
1 (8-ounce) can unsweetened pineapple
   chunks, drained
1 serrano chile, seeded, finely chopped

SALMON FILLETS

1/4 cup chopped fresh cilantro
1/4 cup chopped fresh mint
1 teaspoon vegetable oil
1/8 teaspoon ground red pepper
1/2 teaspoon salt
1/4 teaspoon black pepper
4 (6-ounce) 1-inch-thick salmon fillets
Salt and pepper to taste

For the SALSA, combine the mango, banana, mint, orange juice, lime zest, lime juice, pineapple and chile in a bowl and mix well. Chill, covered, in the refrigerator.

For the SALMON, combine the cilantro, mint, oil, red pepper, 1/2 teaspoon salt and 1/4 teaspoon black pepper in a large sealable plastic bag. Add the salmon and seal the bag. Shake gently to coat the salmon. Marinate in the refrigerator for 20 minutes; drain. Sprinkle the salmon with salt and pepper to taste. Place on a grill rack coated with cooking spray. Cook for 5 minutes on each side or until the salmon flakes easily with a fork. Place the salmon on a platter and top with mango salsa.

Yield: 4 servings

FOIL-BAKED SEA BASS WITH SPINACH

1½ tablespoons butter, at room temperature
1 (5-ounce) bag prewashed baby spinach
Salt and freshly ground pepper
1 shallot, minced

4 (8-ounce) skinless sea bass fillets
¼ cup (½ stick) unsalted butter, cut into
  small pieces
¼ cup dry white wine

Tear off four 18-inch lengths of foil. Brush room-temperature butter over an 8-inch square in the center of each foil sheet. Divide the spinach equally and mound in the center of each sheet. Season with salt, pepper and shallot. Season both sides of the sea bass with salt and pepper and place one fillet on each spinach mound. Scatter the butter pieces over the sea bass. Fold the sides of the foil up around the fish and drizzle with the wine. Seal the packets and place on a baking sheet. Bake at 425 degrees for 12 minutes or until the fish flakes easily with a fork.

Place a packet in a medium bowl. Make a small tear in the side and pour the juices into the bowl. Place the sea bass and spinach from the packet on a shallow soup plate. Repeat with the remaining packets. Pour the cooking juices evenly over the sea bass and serve.

Yield: 4 servings

GRILLED TILAPIA WITH MANGO SALSA

1 (15-ounce) can black beans
1 pint grape tomatoes, chopped
2 mangoes, chopped
2 shallots, chopped
Juice of 3 limes
1 cup chopped fresh cilantro

Black pepper to taste
1½ teaspoons chili powder
1 teaspoon ground cumin
Kosher salt to taste
4 skinless tilapia fillets
Cooked yellow rice

Combine the beans, tomatoes, mangoes, shallots, lime juice and cilantro in a bowl and mix well. Let stand at room temperature.

Combine the pepper, chili powder, cumin and salt in a bowl and mix well. Rub over the tilapia. Grill the tilapia at medium-high on a fish cage or plate until the tilapia flakes easily with a fork. Place the tilapia on a serving platter and top with the salsa. Serve with yellow rice.

Yield: 4 servings

PECAN-CRUSTED TILAPIA

1/2 cup finely ground pecans
2 tablespoons Italian-style bread crumbs
1/2 cup pecan chips
3/4 teaspoon salt
1/4 teaspoon garlic powder
1/2 teaspoon pepper

1 cup milk
1 tablespoon vinegar
1/2 teaspoon Tabasco sauce
1/2 cup all-purpose flour
4 (6-ounce) tilapia fillets
2 tablespoons olive oil

Mix the ground pecans, bread crumbs, pecan chips, salt, garlic powder and pepper in a shallow dish. Combine the milk and vinegar in a shallow bowl. Add the Tabasco sauce and mix well. Place the flour in a shallow dish. Dredge the tilapia in the flour. Dip into the milk mixture. Roll in the pecan mixture until coated.

Heat the olive oil in a large skillet over medium heat. Place the tilapia in the skillet. Cook for 5 minutes on each side or until the pecans are browned and the fish flakes easily with a fork.

Yield: 4 servings

REAL JOY COMES not from ease or riches or from the praise of men, but from doing something worthwhile.

—*Sir Wilfred Grenfell*

SHRIMP AND BUTTERNUT SQUASH IN COCONUT MILK BROTH

This is a great, quick Thai-inspired stew that has a real comfort factor.

3/4 cup lower sodium chicken broth
1 1/2 teaspoons brown sugar
1 teaspoon kosher salt
2 teaspoons tomato paste
1/4 teaspoon crushed red pepper
1/4 teaspoon freshly ground black pepper
1 (14-ounce) can light coconut milk
2 cups (3/4-inch cubes) butternut squash

1 cup julienned red bell pepper
1 pound large shrimp, peeled, deveined, halved lengthwise
2 cups cooked jasmine rice
1/4 cup freshly squeezed lime juice (about 2 to 3 limes)
3 tablespoons minced fresh cilantro

Whisk the broth, brown sugar, salt, tomato paste, red pepper, black pepper and coconut milk in a large saucepan. Add the squash and bell pepper. Bring to a boil. Reduce the heat. Simmer for 10 minutes or until the squash is tender. Purée using a hand-held blender. Stir in the shrimp. Bring to a boil. Cook for 1 minute or until the shrimp turn pink. Stir in the rice, lime juice and cilantro.

Yield: 4 servings

SHRIMP AND VEGGIE KABOBS WITH LEMON PEPPER MARINADE

Serve this over rice for an entrée, or use small skewers and serve as an appetizer.

2 pounds cooked extra-large shrimp	2/3 cup olive oil
1 yellow squash	Juice of 2 lemons
1 zucchini	1 teaspoon sugar
1 yellow bell pepper	Cracked pepper to taste
1 red bell pepper	Salt to taste
1 green bell pepper	Dash of basil
2 Vidalia onions	Dash of oregano

Place the shrimp in a shallow dish. Cut the yellow squash, zucchini, bell peppers and onions into large slices. Add to the shrimp. Combine the olive oil, lemon juice, sugar, cracked pepper, salt, basil and oregano in a separate bowl and mix well. Pour over the shrimp mixture. Chill for 1 hour; drain.

Thread the vegetables and shrimp alternately onto 12 kabob skewers. Place the skewers on a broiler pan. Broil for 5 to 8 minutes or until the vegetables begin to blacken, turning once.

If you use wooden kabob skewers, soak them in water before threading the vegetables and shrimp onto them to prevent burning.

Yield: 6 servings

Sides

Photo: Roasted Vegetables

ROASTED VEGETABLES

2 tablespoons olive oil
5 cups chopped asparagus, onions, squash,
   potatoes, sweet potatoes, carrots and
   brussels sprouts or vegetables of choice
Salt and freshly ground pepper

Drizzle olive oil over a foil-lined jelly roll pan. Spread the vegetables evenly over the bottom of the prepared pan. Sprinkle with salt and pepper. Roast at 450 degrees for 10 to 12 minutes or until tender.

Yield: 6 servings

This recipe is pictured on page 93.

RATATOUILLE

Serve this stewed vegetable dish as a hearty side dish or as an appetizer spread on toasted bread rounds.

1 eggplant, peeled, chopped
1 large onion, chopped
2 zucchini, sliced
6 tomatoes, peeled and chopped, or
   2 (14-ounce) cans crushed
   tomatoes, drained
1/8 teaspoon oregano
1/8 teaspoon basil

3 large garlic cloves, crushed
1 tablespoon sugar
1 tablespoon white vinegar
1/3 cup olive oil
1/2 cup water
Salt and pepper to taste
25 pitted ripe olives, sliced (optional)

Combine the eggplant, onion, zucchini, tomatoes, oregano, basil, garlic, sugar, vinegar, olive oil, water, salt and pepper in a large skillet. Cook, covered, over low heat for 1 hour or until the vegetables are tender, stirring occasionally. Stir in the olives. Cook for 10 minutes or until the liquid is reduced. Serve warm or at room temperature.

Yield: 8 servings

STUFFED ARTICHOKES

1/4 cup (1/2 stick) butter, at room temperature
1/2 cup dry bread crumbs
1/4 cup grated Parmesan cheese
1/2 cup chopped fresh parsley
1/4 cup chopped fresh chives
1 tablespoon grated onion or shallots
1/2 garlic clove, grated
4 artichokes, leaf tips and stems trimmed
Olive oil
Melted butter

Mix 1/4 cup butter, bread crumbs, cheese, parsley, chives, onion and garlic in a bowl. Open the artichoke leaves and spoon the stuffing into every pocket across the top, filling the artichokes with stuffing. Place artichokes in a clay baker or large pan. Add water to a depth of 1 inch. Drizzle the top of the artichokes with olive oil. Bake, covered, at 350 degrees for 75 to 90 minutes or until the artichokes are tender. Serve with a small dish of melted butter for dipping the artichoke leaves.

Yield: 4 servings

GRILLED ASPARAGUS WITH GORGONZOLA BUTTER

3/4 cup loosely packed crumbled
   Gorgonzola cheese
6 tablespoons butter, at room temperature
1 teaspoon freshly squeezed lemon juice
Salt and pepper to taste

2 pounds asparagus, trimmed
2 tablespoons olive oil
1 tablespoon chopped fresh basil
3 garlic cloves, minced

Combine the cheese, butter and lemon juice in a bowl and mix well. Season with salt and pepper. May chill, covered, for up to 2 days.

Arrange the asparagus in a single layer in a baking dish. Whisk the olive oil, basil and garlic in a small bowl. Pour over the asparagus and turn the asparagus to coat. Sprinkle with salt and pepper. Place the asparagus on a grill rack over high heat. Grill for 4 minutes or until charred on all sides, turning occasionally. Arrange on plates and top with Gorgonzola butter.

Yield: 6 servings

PARMESAN ROASTED ASPARAGUS

2 pounds fresh asparagus, trimmed
2 tablespoons olive oil

Salt and pepper to taste
1/4 cup freshly grated Parmesan cheese

Place the asparagus on a rimmed baking sheet. Drizzle with olive oil and turn the asparagus to coat. Arrange in a single layer. Season with salt and pepper. Roast at 400 degrees for 15 minutes or until tender-crisp. Sprinkle with the cheese. Roast for 5 minutes or until the cheese is melted. Cooking times will vary based on the thickness of the asparagus spears.

Yield: 4 to 6 servings

SESAME ASPARAGUS

24 fresh asparagus spears, trimmed
1 teaspoon salt
1 tablespoon plus 1 teaspoon butter
   or margarine

1 tablespoon plus 1 teaspoon lemon juice
1 tablespoon sesame seeds, toasted

Place the asparagus in a skillet and sprinkle with salt. Add water to a depth of 1/2 inch. Bring to a boil. Reduce the heat. Simmer, covered, for 4 minutes or until tender-crisp. Drain and place on a serving platter.

Heat the butter in a saucepan until melted. Stir in the lemon juice and sesame seeds. Drizzle over the asparagus.

Yield: 4 servings

SESAME NOODLES

12 ounces linguini or spaghetti
3 tablespoons sesame seeds, toasted
3 tablespoons vegetable oil
2 tablespoons sesame oil

1 garlic clove, crushed
1/4 cup soy sauce
1/4 cup chopped cilantro
Salt to taste

Cook the linguini according to the package directions. Remove from the heat and let stand for 6 minutes; drain. Combine the sesame seeds, vegetable oil, sesame oil, garlic and soy sauce in a bowl and mix well. Pour over the noodles and toss to combine. Sprinkle with cilantro. Season with salt. Serve hot or cold.

Yield: 4 to 6 servings

TOASTING SESAME SEEDS—Sesame seeds can be toasted on the stovetop or in the oven. On the stove, place the seeds in a dry skillet over medium heat, shaking frequently so that the seeds toast evenly. Alternatively, place the seeds on a baking sheet in a 375-degree oven for 10 to 12 minutes. The seeds will turn a rich brown color around the edges. Watch carefully because the seeds can burn quickly.

SAUTÉED BRUSSELS SPROUTS WITH TOASTED PECANS

2 teaspoons butter
1 cup chopped onion
4 garlic cloves, thinly sliced
8 cups thinly sliced brussels sprouts

1/2 cup chicken broth
1 1/2 tablespoons sugar
1/2 teaspoon salt
8 teaspoons chopped pecans, toasted

Heat the butter in a large skillet over medium heat until melted. Add the onion and garlic. Sauté for 4 minutes or until lightly browned. Stir in the brussels sprouts and sauté for 2 minutes. Add the broth and sugar. Cook for 5 minutes or until the liquid is almost evaporated, stirring frequently. Stir in the salt. Sprinkle with the pecans.

Yield: 8 servings

FETA GREEN BEANS

LEMON VINAIGRETTE
3 tablespoons freshly squeezed lemon juice
3 tablespoons white wine vinegar
1 1/2 tablespoons Dijon mustard
1/2 tablespoon sugar
1/2 cup olive oil
1/4 teaspoon salt
1/4 teaspoon pepper

GREEN BEANS
Salt
1 1/2 pounds green beans
1/2 small red onion, minced
4 ounces crumbled feta cheese

For the VINAIGRETTE, whisk the lemon juice, vinegar, mustard and sugar together in a bowl. Add the olive oil in a fine stream, whisking constantly. Whisk in the salt and pepper.

For the BEANS, bring enough water to cover the beans to a boil in a saucepan. Add a small amount of salt. Add the beans. Cook for 5 minutes. Drain and rinse with ice water. Pat dry. Chill thoroughly, covered, in the refrigerator.

Place the beans in a shallow serving bowl. Add the onion and vinaigrette and toss to combine. Sprinkle with the cheese. Serve chilled or at room temperature.

Yield: 6 to 8 servings

GREEN BEANS WITH CARAMELIZED ONIONS

The sweetened caramelized onions complement the green beans beautifully. These are great for holiday dinners—an elegant alternative to the traditional green bean casserole.

4 onions, cut into thin wedges
3 tablespoons butter
Salt and pepper to taste
1 1/3 cups canned low-sodium chicken broth

2 tablespoons sugar
4 teaspoons red wine vinegar
2 pounds green beans
1 tablespoon butter

Arrange the onions in a single layer on a baking sheet sprayed with nonstick cooking spray. Dot with 3 tablespoons butter. Season with salt and pepper. Bake at 350 degrees for 35 minutes or until the onions are dark brown.

Bring the broth to a boil in a saucepan. Boil for 6 minutes or until reduced to 1/2 cup. Add the sugar and vinegar. Whisk until the sugar dissolves and the mixture comes to a boil. Add the onions. Simmer for 5 minutes. Season with salt and pepper. You may prepare this up to 1 day in advance and reheat.

Bring enough water to cover the green beans to a boil in a saucepan. Add the beans and cook until tender-crisp; drain. Toss the beans with 1 tablespoon butter. Place the beans in a large shallow serving dish. Top with the onion mixture.

Yield: 6 to 8 servings

HOLIDAY MASHED POTATOES

3 pounds potatoes, peeled, cooked, hot
8 ounces cream cheese, at room temperature
1/4 cup (1/2 stick) butter
1/2 cup sour cream
2 eggs, lightly beaten

1/4 cup finely chopped onion
1/2 cup milk
1 teaspoon salt
Dash of pepper
Finely chopped fresh chives

Mash the potatoes in a large mixing bowl. Cut the cream cheese and butter into small pieces. Beat into the potatoes. Add the sour cream and mix well. Combine the eggs, onion and milk in a separate bowl and mix well. Pour into the potato mixture. Add the salt and pepper. Beat the potato mixture until fluffy. Spoon into a 9-inch round baking dish. Chill, covered, for 12 hours or longer. Bake at 350 degrees for 45 minutes. Garnish with chives.

Yield: 6 to 8 servings

CREAMED SPINACH

2 (10-ounce) bags fresh spinach
1 tablespoon olive oil
3 tablespoons minced shallots
1/4 teaspoon salt

1/8 teaspoon nutmeg
3 tablespoons milk
4 ounces cream cheese

Steam the spinach in a steamer for 4 minutes or until wilted; drain. Heat the olive oil in a skillet until hot. Add the shallots. Sauté over medium heat until tender. Reduce the heat to low. Stir in the salt and nutmeg. Add the milk and cream cheese. Cook until the cream cheese is melted, stirring constantly. Add the spinach and mix well.

Yield: 4 to 6 servings

SPINACH WITH SUN-DRIED TOMATOES AND PINE NUTS

1 tablespoon olive oil
1 tablespoon pine nuts
2 garlic cloves, chopped
1/2 teaspoon salt
1/4 teaspoon black pepper
1/4 teaspoon red pepper flakes (optional)
2 tablespoons chopped dried
   sun-dried tomatoes
10 ounces fresh spinach

Heat the olive oil in a skillet over medium-low heat. Add the pine nuts and garlic. Cook until lightly browned. Add the salt, black pepper, red pepper flakes, sun-dried tomatoes and spinach. Cook for 5 to 6 minutes or until the spinach is wilted, stirring occasionally.

Yield: 4 servings

SOCIAL—All work and no play makes Shelly...and Megan and Jackie...no fun. The women of HJWC devote a lot of time and energy to making our annual fund-raising benefit a huge success and helping the community through numerous service projects. But we also have a lot of fun. Our meetings always feature an array of delicious appetizers and tempting desserts. Wine is poured and conversations flow. The club also hosts various social gatherings throughout the year—such as golf outings, bowling parties, and open houses. The friendships made through the club have made our lives richer and spirits lighter—and, as former HJWC members have told us, are friendships that will last a lifetime.

SWEET POTATO BAKE

This is a favorite side dish for holiday meals. Don't plan on many leftovers.

6 sweet potatoes, peeled
1/4 cup (1/2 stick) melted butter
1/4 cup all-purpose flour
2 eggs
1 teaspoon vanilla extract
1/4 cup milk
1/3 cup packed brown sugar

1/4 cup granulated sugar
1 teaspoon grated orange zest
2 teaspoons orange juice
1 cup finely chopped pecans
3/4 cup packed brown sugar
1/2 cup (1 stick) butter
1/3 cup all-purpose flour

Cut the potatoes into 2-inch cubes. Bring enough water to cover the potatoes to a boil in a saucepan. Add the potatoes. Cook until tender; drain. Mash the potatoes in a bowl.

Add the melted butter, 1/4 cup flour, eggs, vanilla, milk, 1/3 cup brown sugar, granulated sugar, orange zest and orange juice to the potatoes and mix well. Spoon into a greased 2-quart baking dish.

Combine the pecans, 3/4 cup brown sugar, butter and 1/3 cup flour in a bowl and mix well. Sprinkle over the top of the potatoes. Bake at 350 degrees for 35 to 40 minutes or until bubbly.

Yield: 6 to 8 servings

BAKED MACARONI AND CHEESE

8 ounces macaroni	Dash of pepper
1 tablespoon butter	1 teaspoon dry mustard
1 egg, beaten	1 tablespoon hot water
1 cup chopped tomatoes (optional)	1 cup milk
3 cups shredded sharp Cheddar cheese	Shredded sharp Cheddar cheese
1 teaspoon salt	

Cook the macaroni according to the package directions. Drain and rinse under cold water. Mix the cooked macaroni, butter, egg and tomatoes in a bowl. Stir in 3 cups cheese. Spoon into a buttered baking dish.

Combine the salt, pepper, dry mustard, hot water and milk in a separate bowl and mix well. Pour over the macaroni mixture. Sprinkle with cheese. Bake at 375 degrees for 45 minutes.

Yield: 6 servings

LEMON ORZO WITH FRESH HERBS

5 cups chicken broth	2 teaspoons lemon juice
1 pound orzo	1 tablespoon chopped fresh basil
2 teaspoons grated lemon zest	1 tablespoon chopped fresh Italian parsley
2 teaspoons peanut oil	1 tablespoon fresh dill weed

Bring the broth to a boil in a saucepan. Add the orzo and cook until al dente. Stir in the lemon zest, peanut oil, lemon juice, basil, parsley and dill weed.

Yield: 6 servings

Desserts

Photo: Stuffed Strawberries

STUFFED STRAWBERRIES

Luscious strawberries and sweet cream cheese filling—these are simply decadent.

2 dozen medium to large strawberries
8 ounces cream cheese, at room temperature
3/4 cup confectioners' sugar
1 teaspoon almond extract
3 tablespoons finely chopped chocolate pieces

Cut a thin slice from the stem of each strawberry, forming a base for it to stand on. Cut two slices forming four wedges, starting at the pointed end; do not cut all the way through the stem.

Beat the cream cheese in a mixing bowl until fluffy. Beat in the confectioners' sugar and almond extract. Stir in the chocolate. Spoon into a pastry bag. Pipe 1 tablespoon into each strawberry. You may prepare the filling 1 day in advance. Do not fill the strawberries more than 4 hours in advance.

Yield: 24 strawberries

This recipe is pictured on page 105.

TWO-BITE CHEESECAKES WITH FRESH BERRIES

These dainty cheesecakes topped with fresh berries and a sprinkling of confectioners' sugar are a beautiful addition to any dessert table.

1/4 cup chopped walnuts
1 3/4 cups crushed graham crackers
1/2 teaspoon cinnamon
1/2 cup (1 stick) melted butter
12 ounces cream cheese,
   at room temperature
1 cup granulated sugar
2 tablespoons all-purpose flour

1 teaspoon vanilla extract
1/2 teaspoon grated lemon zest
2 eggs
1 egg yolk
1/4 cup milk
Fresh raspberries and blueberries
Confectioners' sugar

Grind the walnuts in a food processor. Combine with the graham crackers, cinnamon and butter in a bowl and mix well. Press over the bottoms of 24 to 36 mini-tart pan cups. Bake at 375 degrees for 10 minutes.

Beat the cream cheese, granulated sugar, flour, vanilla and lemon zest in a mixing bowl until fluffy. Beat in the eggs, egg yolk and milk. Spoon into the baked shells. Bake for 35 to 40 minutes or until set. Let stand until completely cooled. Remove and place each cheesecake in a petite paper baking cup. Top with fresh raspberries and blueberries. Dust with confectioners' sugar.

Yield: 24 to 36 cheesecakes

ICED LEMON CREAM AND BLACK RASPBERRY SAUCE

This delicious and surprisingly easy recipe will make your friends think you went to cooking school.

LEMON CREAM
1 cup whipping cream
1 cup half-and-half
1/4 cup lemon juice
Zest from 1/2 lemon
1 cup sugar
Fresh mint (optional)

BLACK RASPBERRY SAUCE
1 1/2 cups mashed black raspberries
1/2 cup packed light brown sugar
2 tablespoons lemon juice
1/2 teaspoon cinnamon
1/8 teaspoon nutmeg

For the **LEMON CREAM**, combine the whipping cream, half-and-half, lemon juice, lemon zest and sugar in a bowl. Mix for 1 minute or until the sugar is dissolved. Pour into a 5×9-inch loaf pan. Freeze, covered, until firm.

For the **SAUCE**, combine the raspberries, brown sugar, lemon juice, cinnamon and nutmeg in a saucepan. Cook over medium heat until hot and bubbly, stirring occasionally. Let stand until cooled.

Scoop the frozen lemon cream and place in dessert bowls. Spoon the sauce over the top.

Yield: 4 to 6 servings

MINT ICE CREAM DESSERT

20 chocolate sandwich cookies
3 squares bittersweet chocolate
1 cup (2 sticks) butter
3 eggs

2 cups confectioners' sugar
1/4 cup crème de menthe
1/2 gallon vanilla ice cream, softened

Place the cookies in a sealable plastic bag and seal the bag. Roll a rolling pin over the cookies until crushed. Sprinkle three-fourths of the crumbs over the bottom of a 9×13-inch baking pan.

Place the chocolate and butter in a microwave-safe bowl. Heat until the chocolate and butter are melted. Let stand until cooled. Add the eggs and beat until thickened. Beat in the confectioners' sugar. Pour over the cookie crumbs. Freeze for 30 minutes or longer. Combine the crème de menthe and ice cream in a bowl and mix well. Spread over the frozen crust. Sprinkle with the remaining cookie crumbs. Freeze, covered, for 12 hours or longer.

You may substitute mint chocolate chip ice cream for the vanilla ice cream and crème de menthe.

NOTE: If you are concerned about using raw eggs, use eggs pasteurized in their shells, which are sold at some specialty food stores, or use an equivalent amount of pasteurized egg substitute.

Yield: 12 servings

HOMEMADE HOT FUDGE SAUCE

1/2 cup sugar
1/4 cup cream
1/2 cup corn syrup
1 1/2 tablespoons butter

Pinch of salt
1/2 teaspoon vanilla extract
1/4 cup cocoa

Combine the sugar, cream, corn syrup, butter, salt and vanilla in a saucepan. Cook until the butter is melted, stirring frequently. Stir in the cocoa. Bring to a boil and boil for 2 minutes, stirring constantly. Serve warm over ice cream, brownies, or other desserts of choice.

Yield: 2 cups

STEAMED HONEYED PEARS

When pears are in season, indulge in this special dessert—a perfect ending to any meal.

6 pears
Cinnamon
Honey

Remove the stems from the pears. Core the pears from the stem end, leaving the base intact. Set the pears upright on a steamer rack. Place a pinch of cinnamon in the cavity of each pear. Fill the pears with honey. Steam for 20 to 30 minutes or until tender. Serve warm.

Yield: 6 servings

APPLE CRISP

4 cups sliced peeled apples
1 teaspoon cinnamon
1/2 teaspoon salt
1/4 cup water
3/4 cup all-purpose flour
1 cup sugar
6 tablespoons butter, softened

Arrange the apples in a buttered 6×10-inch baking pan. Sprinkle with cinnamon, salt and water. Combine the flour, sugar and butter in a bowl and mix until crumbly. Sprinkle over the apples. Bake at 350 degrees for 40 minutes.

Yield: 8 servings

APPLE COBBLER

3 tablespoons butter
2 pounds Golden Delicious apples,
  peeled, sliced
1/2 cup raisins
1/4 cup sugar
1/4 teaspoon cinnamon
1/8 teaspoon nutmeg

1/2 cup (1 stick) butter, melted
1 cup sugar
1 cup all-purpose flour
2 teaspoons baking powder
1 teaspoon salt
1/2 cup milk
Vanilla ice cream or whipped cream

Heat 3 tablespoons butter in a skillet until melted. Add the apples and raisins. Cook over medium heat until tender, stirring occasionally. Stir in 1/4 cup sugar, cinnamon and nutmeg. Remove from the heat.

Pour the melted butter into a 7×11-inch baking dish. Combine 1 cup sugar, flour, baking powder and salt in a bowl and mix well. Stir in the milk. Pour over the butter. Pour the apple mixture over the batter. Bake at 350 degrees for 50 minutes or until the crust is golden brown. Serve warm with vanilla ice cream.

Yield: 6 to 8 servings

BERRY PIE

This festive pie is the perfect dessert for your Fourth of July barbecue. The variations on this versatile recipe are as endless as your choice of an individual berry or a combination of berries. To make this extra special, top it off with some fresh berries and a dollop of homemade whipped cream.

2 1/2 to 3 cups fresh berries, such as
    raspberries, strawberries, blueberries and
    blackberries
1 baked pie shell
1 cup mashed berries

1 cup sugar
2 1/2 tablespoons cornstarch
1/2 cup water
1 tablespoon lemon juice
1 tablespoon butter

Place the fresh berries in the pie shell. Cook the mashed berries, sugar, cornstarch and water in a saucepan over medium heat until the sauce is clear, stirring frequently. Add the lemon juice and butter. Stir until the butter is melted. Pour over the berries in the pie shell. Chill, covered, in the refrigerator.

Yield: 8 servings

This recipe is pictured on the back cover.

SOUTHERN PECAN PIE

2 tablespoons all-purpose flour
1 cup white corn syrup
1 cup packed dark brown sugar
1/3 cup melted butter

2 cups ground pecans
3 eggs, beaten
1 teaspoon vanilla extract
1 unbaked (9-inch) pie shell

Combine the flour, corn syrup, brown sugar, butter, pecans, eggs and vanilla in a bowl and mix well. Pour into the pie shell. Bake at 350 degrees for 1 hour or until set.

Yield: 8 servings

To make your own HOMEMADE WHIPPED CREAM, place one cup chilled heavy cream in a bowl. Beat until firm peaks almost form. Add one teaspoon vanilla extract and one tablespoon sugar. Continue to beat until firm peaks form. Be careful not to overbeat.

RED APPLE CAKE

CAKE
4 red apples, chopped
2 eggs
1/2 cup oil
1/2 teaspoon cinnamon
2 cups sugar
1 cup walnuts, chopped
3/4 teaspoon salt
2 cups all-purpose flour
2 teaspoons baking soda

CREAM CHEESE FROSTING
8 ounces cream cheese, at room temperature
1 teaspoon vanilla extract
1 pound confectioners' sugar
2 teaspoons lemon juice
1/2 cup (1 stick) butter, at room temperature

For the CAKE, combine the apples, eggs, oil, cinnamon, sugar and walnuts in a bowl and mix well. Sift the salt, flour and baking soda together. Add to the apple mixture and mix well. Spoon into a greased 9×13-inch baking pan. Bake at 350 degrees for 55 minutes.

For the FROSTING, combine the cream cheese, vanilla, confectioners' sugar, lemon juice and butter in a bowl and mix well. Spread over the cooled cake. Store the cake, covered, in the refrigerator.

Yield: 36 small or 12 large pieces

DECADENT CHOCOLATE BUNDT CAKE

CAKE
1 package devil's food cake mix
1 (3-ounce) package chocolate instant
   pudding mix
4 eggs
3/4 cup vegetable oil
3/4 cup water
1 cup sour cream
2 cups (12 ounces) semisweet
   chocolate chips

CHOCOLATE ICING
1 cup sugar
5 tablespoons butter
1/3 cup milk
2 cups (12 ounces) semisweet
   chocolate chips

For the CAKE, grease and flour a 12-cup bundt pan. Beat the cake mix, pudding mix, eggs, oil, water and sour cream in a mixing bowl at medium speed for 4 minutes. Stir in the chocolate chips. Pour into the prepared pan. Bake at 350 degrees for 45 to 60 minutes or until a wooden pick inserted in the cake comes out clean. Cool in the pan for 15 minutes or longer. Invert onto a serving plate.

For the ICING, combine the sugar, butter and milk in a medium saucepan over medium heat. Cook for 3 to 4 minutes or until the mixture boils, stirring constantly. Remove from the heat. Add the chocolate chips and stir until the chips are melted. Spread over the cooled cake.

Yield: 8 servings

MINT CHOCOLATE CAKE

This recipe was contributed by Kathleen Johnson Fuller of the historic Fuller family. The delicious chocolate cake and refreshing mint frosting make it a delightful treat!

CAKE
1/2 cup (1 stick) butter, at room temperature
1 cup sugar
4 eggs
1 teaspoon vanilla extract
1 (6-ounce) can chocolate syrup
1 cup plus 1 teaspoon all-purpose flour

FILLING
1/2 cup (1 stick) butter, at room temperature
2 cups confectioners' sugar
1 teaspoon mint extract
2 tablespoons milk
Green food coloring

TOPPING
1 cup (6 ounces) chocolate chips
6 tablespoons butter

For the CAKE, combine the butter, sugar, eggs, vanilla, chocolate syrup and flour in a mixing bowl and beat until smooth and creamy. Pour into a greased 9×13-inch baking pan. Bake at 350 degrees for 30 minutes. Let stand until completely cooled.

For the FILLING, combine the butter, sugar, mint extract, milk and enough food coloring to make of the desired color in a bowl and mix well. Spread over the cake. Chill until the filling is set.

For the TOPPING, heat the chocolate chips and butter in a saucepan until melted. Spread over the filling. Chill until set.

Yield: 12 servings

STRONG FAMILY TIES are the foundation upon which our communities have grown. Although this is a popular area for newly transplanted families to settle, there is a strong base of individuals who grew up and either stayed here all of their lives or ventured out but decided to return to our towns to raise their own families. When the local Hinsdale Hospital counts the 115th Fuller family baby born at their hospital, you know this large family has made its home here for generations. Kathleen Johnson Fuller inherited this recipe from her mother, Myra Johnson, and has proudly served this dessert to her own seven children through the years. It was a special treat for the children at Christmastime and a favorite to bring to school functions to share with friends. She now happily makes it for her eleven grandchildren. Much like this dessert recipe, Mrs. Fuller says that Hinsdale is old-fashioned and family-centric.

CHOCOLATE SOUFFLÉ CAKES WITH CARAMEL SAUCE

CAKES
4 ounces dark chocolate
3/4 cup (1 1/2 sticks) butter
2/3 cup sugar
4 eggs
1/2 cup sifted all-purpose flour

CARAMEL SAUCE
1/4 cup water
1 cup sugar
1/2 cup (1 stick) butter, cut into pieces
1/2 cup heavy cream
2 teaspoons vanilla extract

For the **CAKES**, heat the chocolate and butter in the top of a double boiler over simmering water until melted. Combine the sugar and eggs in a mixing bowl. Beat until the volume begins to increase. Beat in the flour. Beat in the chocolate mixture. Pour into greased 1/2-cup soufflé dishes, leaving 1/2 inch at the top. Chill for 30 minutes. Bake at 400 degrees for 10 to 12 minutes or until the tops rise. Let stand for 2 minutes. Remove from the dish and place on dessert plates.

For the **SAUCE**, combine the water and sugar in a saucepan. Swirl the pan gently over medium-high heat until the sugar is melted and the mixture is clear; do not boil. Cook, covered, for 2 minutes or until the mixture boils. Remove the cover and swirl gently until the mixture becomes dark golden and smokes slightly. Turn off the heat and leave the saucepan on the burner. Whisk in the butter. Whisk in the cream. Cook over low heat and stir constantly if the sauce becomes too thick. Remove from the burner and stir in the vanilla. Spoon over the hot cakes.

NOTE: The caramel sauce alone would be delicious over vanilla ice cream.

Yield: 6 or 7 cakes

POUND CAKE

3 cups all-purpose flour
1/2 teaspoon baking powder
1 teaspoon salt
2 cups (4 sticks) butter, at room temperature
3 cups sugar
8 eggs
2 teaspoons vanilla extract

Grease two loaf pans and line with waxed paper. Combine the flour, baking powder and salt in a bowl and mix well. Cream the butter and sugar in a mixing bowl until light and fluffy. Beat in the eggs and vanilla. Add the dry ingredients in three additions, mixing well after each addition. Beat for 20 minutes at medium speed. Pour into the prepared pans. Bake at 325 degrees for 1 to 1 1/2 hours or until a wooden pick inserted in the cake comes out clean.

Yield: 16 servings

PUMPKIN CAKE

CAKE
2 cups all-purpose flour
1 teaspoon baking soda
1 teaspoon baking powder
1/2 teaspoon salt
4 eggs
1 cup canned pumpkin
1 cup vegetable oil
2 teaspoons cinnamon
2 cups sugar

FROSTING
1 (1-pound) package confectioners' sugar
8 ounces cream cheese, at room temperature
1/4 cup (1/2 stick) butter, at room temperature
2 teaspoons vanilla extract
2 tablespoons milk

For the CAKE, combine the flour, baking soda, baking powder and salt in a bowl and mix well. Beat the eggs in a mixing bowl. Add the pumpkin, oil, cinnamon and sugar and mix well. Add the dry ingredients and stir by hand until smooth. Pour into a large jelly roll pan. Bake at 350 degrees for 20 to 25 minutes or until a wooden pick inserted in the cake comes out clean.

For the FROSTING, beat the confectioners' sugar, cream cheese, butter, vanilla and milk in a mixing bowl. Spread over the cooled cake. Store the cake, covered, in the refrigerator.

Yield: 36 servings

TEXAS SHEET CAKE

CAKE
1 cup water
1 cup (2 sticks) butter
1/4 cup cocoa
2 cups sugar
2 cups all-purpose flour
1 teaspoon baking soda
1/2 teaspoon salt
2 eggs
1/2 cup sour cream

CHOCOLATE FROSTING
6 tablespoons milk
1/4 cup cocoa
1/2 cup (1 stick) butter
1 (1-pound) package confectioners' sugar
1 teaspoon vanilla extract
1 cup chopped nuts (optional)

For the CAKE, bring the water, butter and cocoa to a boil in a saucepan. Remove from the heat. Add the sugar, flour, baking soda and salt and mix well. Combine the eggs and sour cream in a bowl and mix well. Add to the chocolate mixture and mix well. Pour into a greased jelly roll pan. Bake at 375 degrees for 20 minutes. Let stand until cooled.

For the FROSTING, combine the milk, cocoa and butter in a saucepan. Cook until the butter is melted, stirring frequently. Remove from the heat. Add the confectioners' sugar, vanilla and nuts and mix well. Let stand until cooled. Spread over the cooled cake.

Yield: 16 to 20 servings

CHOCOLATE CHIP COOKIES

These chewy and chocolaty cookies will become your new chocolate chip cookie recipe of choice.

1 1/2 cups sifted all-purpose flour
1/2 teaspoon baking soda
1/2 teaspoon salt
2/3 cup butter, at room temperature
1/2 cup granulated sugar

1/2 cup packed brown sugar
1 egg
1 teaspoon vanilla extract
1 cup (6 ounces) semisweet
  chocolate pieces

Sift the flour, baking soda and salt together. Combine the butter, granulated sugar, brown sugar, egg and vanilla in a bowl and mix well. Add the sifted dry ingredients and mix well. Stir in the chocolate pieces. Drop by rounded teaspoonfuls about 2 inches apart onto an ungreased cookie sheet. Bake at 375 degrees for 6 to 10 minutes or until browned; the cookies should still be soft. Cool slightly on the cookie sheet. Remove to a wire rack to cool completely.

Yield: 3 dozen small cookies

ONE CANNOT THINK WELL, love well, sleep well, if one has not dined well.

—Virginia Woolf, *A Room of One's Own*

DOUBLE CHOCOLATE COOKIES

2 cups all-purpose flour
3/4 cup Dutch-processed cocoa
1 teaspoon baking soda
1/2 teaspoon salt
1 1/4 (2 1/2 sticks) cups butter, at room
 temperature

2 cups sugar
2 eggs
2 teaspoons vanilla extract
3/4 cup semisweet chocolate chips
3/4 cup pecans, chopped (optional)
Sugar for coating

Sift the flour, cocoa, baking soda and salt together. Beat the butter, 2 cups sugar and eggs in a mixing bowl using the paddle attachment for 2 minutes or until light and fluffy. Beat in the vanilla. Add the dry ingredients gradually, beating at low speed. Stir in the chocolate chips and pecans. Chill, covered, for 2 hours or until the dough is firm.

Shape the dough into 1-inch balls. Place the sugar for coating in a shallow bowl. Roll each ball in sugar to coat. Place on a nonstick cookie sheet about 1 1/2 inches apart; do not place more than sixteen on a cookie sheet. Bake at 350 degrees for 10 minutes or until set. Cool for 5 minutes on the cookie sheet. Remove to a wire rack to cool completely.

Yield: 5 dozen cookies

OLD-FASHIONED GINGERBREAD MEN

These delicious gingerbread men are just like the ones our grandmothers used to make.

COOKIES
5 cups sifted all-purpose flour
1½ teaspoons baking soda
½ teaspoon salt
2½ teaspoons ginger
1½ teaspoons cinnamon
1 teaspoon ground cloves
1 cup (2 sticks) unsalted butter, at room
  temperature
1 cup sugar

1 jumbo egg
1 cup light molasses
2 tablespoons vinegar

ICING
3 to 4 tablespoons light cream or half-and-
  half
2 cups confectioners' sugar
Food coloring (optional)
Colored sugar crystals (optional)

For the COOKIES, combine the flour, baking soda, salt, ginger, cinnamon and cloves in a bowl and mix well. Cream the butter and sugar in a mixing bowl until light and fluffy. Add the egg, molasses and vinegar and mix well. Add the dry ingredients and mix well. Chill for 3 hours or longer.

Roll the dough ⅛ inch thick on a lightly floured surface. Cut out the gingerbread men with a cookie cutter. Place 1 inch apart on a greased cookie sheet. Bake at 375 degrees for 5 to 6 minutes or until the edges are golden brown. Cool on the cookie sheet. Remove to a wire rack to cool completely.

For the ICING, add enough of the cream to the confectioners' sugar to make of a decorating consistency and mix well. Stir in the food coloring. Spoon into a pastry tube. Pipe the frosting decoratively onto the gingerbread men. You may add additional cream to the icing and spread the icing over the top of the cookies, sprinkling with colored sugar crystals. Let the icing harden completely before stacking the cookies on a plate.

Yield: 4 dozen cookies

"MY GRANDMA WAS BORN in 1890 in Chicago, Illinois. She lived to be 101. When she was little, her parents would take her in a horse and buggy and ride out west from their home in Chicago to visit relatives at Christmastime. She remembered seeing the Victorian homes in LaGrange and Hinsdale as new construction being built out in the 'country.' When I was a child, my grandma would bake a large box of gingerbread cookies for me every Christmas. These cookies taste the way I remember them as a child."

PEANUT BLOSSOM COOKIES

1 3/4 cups all-purpose flour
1/2 cup granulated sugar
1/2 cup packed brown sugar
1 teaspoon baking soda
1/2 teaspoon salt
1/2 cup (1 stick) unsalted butter,
  at room temperature

1/2 cup creamy peanut butter
2 tablespoons milk
1 teaspoon vanilla extract
1 egg
Granulated sugar for coating
36 to 48 chocolate kisses

Combine the flour, 1/2 cup granulated sugar, brown sugar, baking soda, salt, butter, peanut butter, milk, vanilla and egg in a bowl and mix well. Place sugar for coating in a shallow bowl. Shape the dough into tablespoon-size balls. Roll in the granulated sugar. Place on a cookie sheet. Bake at 375 degrees for 10 to 12 minutes or until the edges begin to brown. Top each warm cookie with a kiss. Remove to a wire rack to cool completely.

Yield: 3 to 4 dozen

OLD-FASHIONED SUGAR COOKIES

These delicate round cookies, covered in sugar, are perfect for tea or a child's afternoon snack with hot cocoa.

1 1/2 cups all-purpose flour	1 cup sugar
1 teaspoon baking soda	1 egg
1 teaspoon cream of tartar	1 teaspoon vanilla extract
Pinch of salt	1/2 cup vegetable oil
1/2 cup shortening	Sugar for coating

Sift the flour, baking soda, cream of tartar and salt together. Cream the shortening and 1 cup sugar in a mixing bowl until light and fluffy. Beat in the egg, vanilla and oil. Add the sifted dry ingredients and mix well. Shape into 1-inch balls. Pour the sugar for coating into a shallow bowl. Roll the balls in the sugar to coat. Place on a greased cookie sheet. Flatten with the bottom of a glass dipped in sugar.

Bake at 350 degrees for 10 to 12 minutes or until the edges are lightly browned.

Yield: 18 cookies

SNOW DAYS—At the slightest sprinkling of snow, children scramble to put on their snowsuits and mittens and head out to play. Catching snowflakes on your tongue, making snow angels, and throwing snowballs are just the beginning of the fun. There are snowmen to be made, hills to sled, and snow forts to conquer. The outdoor skating rink at Burns Field in Hinsdale is a popular destination for skaters and hockey players alike. Sitting by a fire with a cup of hot chocolate and warm cookies is the perfect way to end a splendid snowy afternoon.

WHITE CHOCOLATE GRANOLA COOKIES

Although the ingredient list is lengthy, these cookies are so worth the effort!

½ cup chopped dried apricots
1 cup chopped dried cherries
1 cup hot water
2 cups all-purpose flour
¾ teaspoon baking soda
¾ teaspoon cinnamon
1 cup (2 sticks) butter, at room temperature

2¼ cups packed brown sugar
2/3 cup granulated sugar
2 eggs
1½ teaspoons vanilla extract
2¼ cups old-fashioned oats
2 cups white chocolate chunks
1 cup crumbled granola

Place the apricots and cherries in a medium bowl. Cover with hot water and let stand for 15 minutes; drain.

Whisk the flour, baking soda and cinnamon together.

Cream the butter, brown sugar and granulated sugar in a mixing bowl until light and fluffy. Beat in the eggs and vanilla. Add the dry ingredients and mix well. Stir in the oats, chocolate chunks, granola, apricots and cherries. Drop by spoonfuls onto a cookie sheet. Bake at 325 degrees for 15 minutes. Remove to a wire rack to cool.

Yield: 3 dozen cookies

CELEBRITY BROWNIES

These brownies are a star attraction on any dessert table.

2 (1-ounce) squares unsweetened chocolate
1/2 cup (1 stick) butter
1 cup granulated sugar
2 eggs

1/2 teaspoon vanilla extract
1/4 cup all-purpose flour
1/2 teaspoon salt
Confectioners' sugar

Heat the chocolate and butter in a small saucepan until melted, stirring occasionally. Pour into a large bowl. Add the granulated sugar, eggs and vanilla and mix well. Add the flour and salt and mix well. Pour into a buttered and floured 8-inch square pan. Bake at 325 degrees for 35 minutes for chewy brownies or 40 minutes for crispy brownies. Sprinkle the top with confectioners' sugar.

Yield: 24 brownies

CHOCOLATE PEANUT BUTTER SQUARES

1/2 cup (1 stick) butter, at room temperature
1/2 cup peanut butter
1/2 cup granulated sugar
1/2 cup packed brown sugar
1 egg

1 tablespoon water
1 1/4 cups all-purpose flour
3/4 teaspoon baking soda
1/2 teaspoon baking powder
2 1/2 cups (15 ounces) chocolate chips

Combine the butter, peanut butter, granulated sugar, brown sugar and egg in a bowl and mix well. Add the water, flour, baking soda and baking powder and mix well. Stir in 1 1/2 cups of the chocolate chips. Spread over the bottom of a greased 8-inch square pan. Bake at 350 degrees for 20 minutes. Sprinkle with the remaining 1 cup chocolate chips. Bake for 1 minute. Spread the warm chips over the bars, completely covering the top. Chill for 1 hour or until the topping is set. Cut into bite-size squares.

Yield: 36 squares

BANANA BARS

BARS
½ cup (1 stick) butter, at room temperature
1½ cups sugar
2 eggs
1 cup sour cream
1 teaspoon vanilla extract
2 cups all-purpose flour
1 teaspoon baking soda
¼ teaspoon salt
1 cup mashed bananas

FROSTING
8 ounces cream cheese, at room temperature
½ cup (1 stick) butter, at room temperature
2 teaspoons vanilla extract
3¾ to 4 cups confectioners' sugar

For the BARS, cream the butter and sugar in a mixing bowl until light and fluffy. Add the eggs, sour cream and vanilla and mix well. Add the flour, baking soda and salt and mix well. Stir in the bananas. Spread in a greased 10×15-inch jelly roll pan. Bake at 350 degrees for 20 to 25 minutes or until a wooden pick inserted near the center comes out clean. Let stand until cooled.

For the FROSTING, combine the cream cheese and butter in a bowl and mix well. Add the vanilla and mix well. Stir in the confectioners' sugar gradually, adding enough to make of the desired consistency. Spread over the cooled bars.

Yield: 20 servings

LEMON SQUARES

1 cup all-purpose flour	2 teaspoons grated lemon zest (optional)
1/2 cup (1 stick) unsalted butter, at room temperature	2 tablespoons lemon juice
	1/2 teaspoon baking powder
1/4 cup confectioners' sugar	1/4 teaspoon salt
1 cup granulated sugar	2 eggs

Combine the flour, butter and confectioners' sugar in a bowl and mix well. Press evenly over the bottom and 5/8 inch up the sides of an 8-inch square pan. Bake at 350 degrees for 20 minutes.

Beat the granulated sugar, lemon zest, lemon juice, baking powder, salt and eggs in a mixing bowl until light and fluffy. Pour over the hot crust. Bake for 25 minutes or until the top springs back when lightly touched in the center. Let stand until cooled. Cut into 1 1/2-inch squares.

Yield: 25 squares

SCOTCHEROOS

1 cup sugar	6 cups crisp rice cereal
1 cup light corn syrup	1 1/2 cups (9 ounces) chocolate chips
1 cup peanut butter	1 1/2 cups (9 ounces) butterscotch chips

Bring the sugar and corn syrup to a boil in a large saucepan, stirring constantly. Remove from the heat. Stir in the peanut butter. Stir in the cereal quickly. Press over the bottom of a lightly greased 9×13-inch baking pan. Let stand until hardened. Combine the chocolate and butterscotch chips in the top of a double boiler over hot water. Cook until melted, stirring frequently. Spread over the cereal layer. Cut into bars.

Yield: 40 bars

CHOCOLATE CARAMEL GRAHAMS

Pack these scrumptious candy treats in a special tin or cellophane bag tied with grosgrain ribbon for a sweet and adorable holiday gift.

12 (2¹/₂×4³/₄-inch) graham crackers
3/4 cup (1¹/₂ sticks) butter
¹/₂ cup packed brown sugar

1¹/₂ cups (9 ounces) chocolate chips
Chopped nuts, seasonal sprinkles or
   toffee bits (optional)

Line a 10×15-inch rimmed baking sheet with foil, completely covering the bottom and sides. Line the bottom of the prepared pan with graham crackers.

Heat the butter in a saucepan over medium heat until melted. Add the brown sugar. Whisk for 2 minutes or until the mixture is smooth. Pour evenly over the crackers. Bake at 375 degrees for 8 to 10 minutes. Sprinkle the chocolate chips over the top. Bake for 1 minute. Remove from the oven and spread warm chocolate chips evenly over the crackers. Sprinkle with the nuts. Let stand for 20 minutes. Freeze for 15 minutes or until firm. Lift the crackers off the foil and break into pieces.

Yield: 12 servings

CHOCOLATE CHEESECAKE BALLS

1 package chocolate sandwich cookies
8 ounces cream cheese, at room temperature

2 (8-ounce) packages white chocolate
Chocolate sprinkles (optional)

Combine the cookies and cream cheese in a blender and process. Shape into small balls. Chill for 1 hour.

Heat the chocolate in a small saucepan over medium-low heat until melted. Dip each ball into the chocolate to coat, using a wooden pick. Place on waxed paper. Let stand until the chocolate is hardened. Decorate with sprinkles. You may drizzle with dark chocolate for an elegant finish. Store the cheesecake balls, covered, in the refrigerator.

Yield: 3 dozen

HOMEMADE CARAMEL CORN

For a fun retro treat, scoop this homemade candy corn into popcorn bags at your next party and watch them disappear. This is one of our stand-out favorite recipes—just beware, it is addictive.

9 quarts popped popcorn
   (about 2 microwaved bags)
Nuts to taste
2 cups packed brown sugar

1 cup (2 sticks) butter
1/2 teaspoon salt
1/2 cup white corn syrup
1/2 teaspoon baking soda

Spread the popcorn and nuts evenly over a rimmed baking pan. Bring the brown sugar, butter, salt and corn syrup to a boil in a saucepan. Boil for 5 minutes, stirring constantly. Turn off the heat. Add the baking soda and mix well. Pour over the popcorn and nuts. Bake at 250 degrees for 1 hour, stirring every 15 minutes.

Yield: 6 to 8 servings

SUGARED BRANDY BALLS

2 1/2 cups finely crushed vanilla
wafer cookies
1 cup confectioners' sugar
2 tablespoons cocoa

1 cup chopped pecans or walnuts
1/4 cup light corn syrup
1/4 cup brandy or rum
Confectioners' sugar

Combine the cookies, 1 cup confectioners' sugar, cocoa, pecans, corn syrup and brandy in a bowl and mix well. Shape into balls of the desired size, coating hands with confectioners' sugar. Let stand on waxed paper for 1 hour. Store in a sealable plastic bag with additional confectioners' sugar.

Yield: Variable

WHITE CHOCOLATE HOLIDAY MIX

3 cups toasted oat cereal
6 cups Crispix cereal
2 cups pretzel sticks
2 cups red-skinned peanuts

1 large bag candy-coated chocolate pieces
in holiday colors
1 pound white chocolate

Combine the toasted oat cereal, Crispix cereal, pretzel sticks, peanuts and candies in a large bowl and toss to combine. Spread over waxed paper. Heat the chocolate in the top of a double boiler over simmering water until melted, stirring frequently. Pour over the cereal mixture. Let stand until cooled. Break into pieces.

Yield: About 64 (1/4-cup) servings

BREADS
& Breakfast

Photo: Double Melted Banana Bread

DOUBLE MELTED BANANA BREAD

Don't let those brown bananas go to waste. Whip up some of this delicious banana bread.

2 cups all-purpose flour
1 teaspoon baking soda
1/2 teaspoon salt
1/2 cup (1 stick) butter, at room temperature
1 cup sugar
2 eggs

1/2 teaspoon vanilla extract
2 bananas, mashed
1/2 cup cold water
1 1/2 cups finely chopped walnuts
1 cup (6 ounces) chocolate chips (optional)

Mix the flour, baking soda and salt in a bowl. Cream the butter and sugar in a mixing bowl until light and fluffy. Beat in the eggs, vanilla and bananas. Add the dry ingredients and mix just until blended. Stir in the water. Stir in the walnuts and chocolate chips. Pour into a greased 5×9-inch loaf pan. Bake at 350 degrees for 1 hour and 10 minutes. Cool in the pan for 5 minutes. Remove to a wire rack to cool completely.

Yield: 1 loaf

This recipe is pictured on page 133.

"MY GRANDMA GREW UP in the country. Every time she came to visit, she'd bring loaves of this banana bread. We'd anxiously look forward to her special treat. Now I make these with my children—carrying forward the family tradition."

APRICOT TEA BREAD

½ cup dried apricots
½ cup raisins
1 cup freshly squeezed orange juice
   (about 1 or 2 oranges)
1 teaspoon baking soda
2 teaspoons baking powder
¼ teaspoon salt

2 cups all-purpose flour
2 tablespoons butter
1 cup sugar
1 egg
½ teaspoon vanilla extract
2 teaspoons orange flavoring
½ cup chopped nuts

Soak the apricots in water to cover in a bowl for 30 minutes; drain. Chop the apricots and raisins finely. Combine the orange juice and baking soda in a bowl. Stir in the apricots and raisins.

Sift the baking powder, salt and flour together. Cream the butter and sugar in a mixing bowl until light and fluffy. Add the egg, vanilla and orange flavoring and mix well. Add the sifted dry ingredients and mix well. Stir in the apricot mixture and the nuts. Pour into a greased loaf pan. Bake at 350 degrees for 1 hour.

Yield: 1 loaf

SWEET ORANGE TEA BREAD

This delicate bread with candied orange peel throughout is reminiscent of the days of afternoon tea and lace doilies.

Rind of 2 oranges	1 teaspoon salt
4 cups water	1/3 cup butter, at room temperature
1 cup sugar	1 cup sugar
3 cups all-purpose flour	1 egg
2 teaspoons baking powder	1 cup milk

Bring the orange rind and water to a boil in a saucepan. Boil until the rind is tender. Drain, reserving the water. Scrape the fiber from the rind and discard. Chop the rind finely. Combine 1 cup sugar, chopped rind and reserved water in a saucepan. Bring to a boil. Boil to the thickness of marmalade, about 1 generous cup, stirring frequently.

Sift the flour, baking powder and salt together. Cream the butter and sugar in a mixing bowl until light and fluffy. Beat in the egg and milk. Add the sifted dry ingredients and mix well. Stir in the orange rind mixture. Pour into a greased large loaf pan. Bake at 350 degrees for 1 hour and 10 minutes. You may bake in two small loaf pans for 1 hour.

Yield: 1 large loaf

THERE ARE BEAUTIFUL HOMES in Hinsdale and its surrounding towns that come in all shapes and sizes. There are homes dating to the time of the early settlers and brand new homes constructed each day. Some of the more interesting homes in the area are the English Cotswold cottage-style homes designed by Hinsdale's most celebrated architect, R. Harold Zook, in the early twentieth century. With their distinctive "thatched" roofs, beamed cathedral ceilings, and spider web designs, they have been compared to fairy tale cottages. When Mr. Zook's Hinsdale home and studio was being threatened with demolition, local preservationists rallied the community to save the home. In May of 2005, hundreds of people watched as the buildings were lifted onto trucks and slowly moved over two days through the streets of Hinsdale to their new home in Katherine Legge Memorial Park.

CRANBERRY BREAD

2 cups all-purpose flour
1 cup sugar
½ teaspoon salt
½ teaspoon baking soda
1½ teaspoons baking powder
1 egg, well beaten

½ cup orange juice
2 tablespoons melted butter
2 tablespoons hot water
½ cup pecans
1½ cups cranberries, cut into halves

Grease a loaf pan with unsalted shortening. Combine the flour, sugar, salt, baking soda and baking powder in a large bowl and mix well. Combine the egg, orange juice and butter in a separate bowl and mix well. Add hot water, pecans and cranberries and mix well. Add to the flour mixture and mix well. Pour into the prepared pan. Bake at 350 degrees for 1 hour and 10 minutes. You may pulse the cranberries briefly in a food processor instead of cutting them into halves.

Yield: 1 loaf

HARVEST BREAD

3 cups sugar
1 cup oil
4 eggs
2 cups canned pumpkin
3½ cups all-purpose flour
1½ teaspoons cinnamon
1½ teaspoons allspice

1 teaspoon nutmeg
½ teaspoon salt
2 teaspoons baking soda
⅔ cup water
1½ cups chopped nuts (optional)
1½ cups (9 ounces) chocolate chips

Beat the sugar, oil, eggs and pumpkin in a mixing bowl at low speed until blended. Combine the flour, cinnamon, allspice, nutmeg and salt in a separate bowl and mix well. Dissolve the baking soda in the water in a small bowl. Add the flour mixture alternately with the baking soda mixture to the pumpkin mixture, mixing well after each addition. Stir in the nuts and chocolate chips. Pour into three greased loaf pans. Bake at 350 degrees for 50 to 60 minutes or until a wooden pick inserted near the center comes out clean. You may also bake this in a greased bundt pan for 60 to 75 minutes.

Yield: 3 loaves

GRAUE MILL CORN BREAD

1 cup all-purpose flour
1 tablespoon baking powder
1 cup milk
1 egg
1 cup cornmeal
⅓ cup sugar
¼ cup (½ stick) butter, melted
1 teaspoon salt

Sift the flour and baking powder together. Add the milk and egg and mix well. Stir in the cornmeal. Add the sugar, butter and salt and mix well. Pour into a greased 8-inch square pan. Bake at 425 degrees for 20 minutes. You may also bake in miniature muffin tins for 12 to 14 minutes or muffin tins for 18 minutes.

Yield: 8 servings

GRAUE MILL, located within the popular nature attraction, Fullersburg Woods Forest Preserve, is the only operating waterwheel gristmill in the state of Illinois. The mill, constructed in 1852, was used to grind the wheat, corn, and other grains produced by local farmers for over sixty years. Steeped in history, the mill once harbored slaves on the Underground Railroad. The mill was a major technology center for economic activity in the nineteenth century and was reportedly visited by Abraham Lincoln during a trip from Chicago to Springfield, Illinois.

The Graue Mill and Museum provide educational programs to schoolchildren and the public, including milling, spinning, and weaving, as well as a historical perspective on the Mill and its place in history. Listed on the National Register of Historic Places in May 1975, Graue Mill continues to be a treasure of the historic western suburbs of Chicago.

GRAUE MILL CORNMEAL GRIDDLE CAKES

2 cups all-purpose flour
1 tablespoon sugar
1 teaspoon salt
1 tablespoon baking powder
1/2 cup cornmeal
1 1/2 cups milk
2 egg yolks
1/4 cup (1/2 stick) butter, melted
2 egg whites

Combine the flour, sugar, salt, baking powder and cornmeal in a bowl and mix well. Add the milk and mix well. Stir in the egg yolks and butter. Beat the egg whites in a mixing bowl until stiff peaks form. Fold into the batter.

Pour 1/4 cup at a time onto a hot griddle. Cook until golden brown on both sides, turning once. Serve warm with maple syrup.

Yield: 10 to 12 pancakes

TRADITIONAL IRISH SODA BREAD

This is undoubtedly the best soda bread you will ever taste. Serve it with some REAL butter . . . your family will thank you.

3 cups all-purpose flour
1 tablespoon baking powder
1 teaspoon baking soda
2/3 cup sugar
1 teaspoon salt

1 cup golden raisins
1 teaspoon oil or melted butter
1 3/4 cups buttermilk
2 eggs, beaten

Mix the flour, baking powder, baking soda, sugar, salt and raisins in a bowl, coating the raisins with the mixture. Add the oil, buttermilk and eggs and mix just until blended. Pour into a greased 10-inch ovenproof skillet or two greased loaf pans. Bake at 350 degrees for 50 to 60 minutes or until the bread tests done.

Yield: 1 (10-inch) skillet of bread or 2 loaves

HOMEMADE CRUSTY BREAD

Forget the bread machine and try this recipe. Making your own homemade bread is not so hard, and think about how proud you'll be when you pull this out of the oven for dinner.

3 (¼-ounce) envelopes dry yeast
2 tablespoons honey
2 cups (or more) tepid water

7 cups (or more) white bread flour
1 tablespoon salt

Dissolve the yeast and honey in 1 cup of the water. Combine the flour and salt in a large microwave-safe bowl and mix well. Microwave for 30 to 60 seconds or until warm. Make a well in the center of the flour mixture. Pour in the yeast mixture. Stir the flour mixture into the yeast mixture gradually with circular movements, beginning at the outer edge of the bowl, until all of the yeast mixture is absorbed. Pour in the remaining 1 cup water and stir to make a moist dough, adding additional water if needed. Knead the dough in the bowl for 5 minutes, adding additional flour if the dough sticks. Dust the top of the dough with flour. Shape into a round and place on a baking sheet. Score the top. Let rise, covered, in a warm place for 40 minutes or until doubled in size.

Punch the dough down. Shape into two French bread-style loaves and place on a baking sheet. Score the tops. Let rise, covered, for 40 minutes or until doubled in size.

Bake at 425 degrees for 35 minutes or until the loaves sound hollow when tapped on the bottom. Serve warm.

Yield: 2 loaves

THREE-CHEESE DROP BISCUITS

1 1/4 cups all-purpose flour
1 1/2 tablespoons sugar
1 teaspoon baking powder
1/4 teaspoon baking soda
1/4 teaspoon salt
3 tablespoons chilled butter, chopped

1/2 cup packed shredded sharp
   Cheddar cheese
1/2 cup packed shredded Monterey
   Jack cheese
1/2 cup grated Parmesan cheese
2/3 cup buttermilk

Whisk the flour, sugar, baking powder, baking soda and salt together in a bowl. Cut in the butter until crumbly. Add the Cheddar cheese, Monterey Jack cheese and Parmesan cheese and mix well. Stir in the buttermilk gradually. Drop dough by 1/4 cups 2 inches apart onto a lightly buttered baking sheet. Bake at 400 degrees for 16 minutes or until golden on top. Serve warm.

Yield: 2 dozen biscuits

CHERRY ALMOND BISCOTTI

2 1/2 cups all-purpose flour
1 cup sugar
1/2 teaspoon baking soda
1/2 teaspoon baking powder
1/2 teaspoon salt

3 eggs
1/2 teaspoon vanilla extract
1/2 teaspoon almond extract
1 cup dried cherries
1 cup slivered almonds

Butter and flour a large baking sheet. Combine the flour, sugar, baking soda, baking powder and salt in a large bowl and mix well. Add the eggs, vanilla and almond extract and beat until well mixed. Stir in the cherries and almonds. Shape into two 2×13-inch logs. Place 2 inches apart on the prepared baking sheet. Bake at 325 degrees for 30 minutes or until golden. Cool on the baking sheet for 10 minutes. Remove to a cutting board.

Cut each log diagonally into 1/2-inch-thick slices. Place the slices sides down on the baking sheet. Bake for 10 minutes. The biscotti may be frozen or stored in an airtight container for several days.

Yield: 2 to 3 dozen

APPLE PUFF SKILLET PANCAKE

Next Sunday morning, make this special treat and delight your family.

3 eggs

3/4 cup all-purpose flour

3/4 cup milk

1/2 teaspoon salt

5 tablespoons sugar

1 teaspoon cinnamon

4 apples, thinly sliced

5 tablespoons butter

Place a 12-inch cast-iron skillet in a 400-degree oven to heat. Beat the eggs in a mixing bowl until frothy. Add the flour, milk and salt and beat for 1 minute. Combine the sugar and cinnamon in a small bowl. Add the apples and toss to coat the apple slices.

Place the butter in the hot skillet and swirl until the butter is melted and the bottom and side of the skillet are coated. Arrange the apples over the bottom of the skillet. Pour the batter over the apples. Bake for 25 minutes or until puffy and golden brown.

Yield: 4 servings

PERFECT PANCAKES

1 egg	2 tablespoons vegetable oil
3/4 cup plus 2 tablespoons milk	1 tablespoon baking powder
1/2 cup all-purpose flour	1/4 teaspoon vanilla extract
1/2 cup whole wheat flour	1/4 teaspoon salt
1 tablespoon brown sugar	1/8 teaspoon cinnamon

Beat the egg in a mixing bowl. Beat in the milk. Add the flour, whole wheat flour, brown sugar, oil, baking powder, vanilla, salt and cinnamon and beat until smooth.

Heat a griddle to 375 degrees. Grease lightly with butter. Pour enough batter onto the griddle to make pancakes of the desired size. Cook until bubbles appear on the surface and the underside is golden brown. Turn the pancake. Cook until the underside is golden brown.

KIDS' FAVORITE: As the pancakes are cooking, add a few miniature candy-coated chocolate pieces or chocolate chips. Or, for banana pancakes, add 1 cup mashed bananas (about 2 medium bananas) to the recipe.

Yield: Variable

This recipe is pictured on page 3.

FROM WHAT WE GET, we can make a living; what we give, however, makes a life.

—*Arthur Ashe*

BAKED FRENCH TOAST ROLL-UPS

This is a fun twist on the classic French toast casserole. Rolling the bread creates an easy to serve, pretty presentation.

5 eggs, lightly beaten
1 1/2 cups milk
1 cup half-and-half
1 teaspoon vanilla extract
1/2 teaspoon cinnamon
16 slices buttered white bread or cinnamon swirl bread

1/2 cup (1 stick) butter, at room temperature
1 cup packed brown sugar
2 tablespoons maple syrup
1 cup chopped pecans

Whisk the eggs, milk, half-and-half, vanilla and cinnamon together in a medium bowl. Dip each bread slice in the egg mixture, roll up and place in a greased 9×13-inch baking dish. Pour the remaining egg mixture over the bread rolls. Chill, covered, for 12 hours or longer.

Combine the butter, brown sugar and maple syrup in a small bowl and mix well. Stir in the pecans. Spread over the bread rolls. Bake at 350 degrees for 40 minutes or until golden.

Yield: 8 servings

BLUEBERRY BUCKLE

FILLING
2 cups all-purpose flour
3/4 cup sugar
2 1/2 teaspoons baking powder
3/4 teaspoon salt
1/4 cup (1/2 stick) butter, at room temperature
3/4 cup milk
1 egg
2 cups blueberries

TOPPING
1/2 cup sugar
1/3 cup all-purpose flour
1/2 teaspoon cinnamon
1/4 cup (1/2 stick) butter, at room temperature

For the **FILLING**, combine the flour, sugar, baking powder, salt, butter, milk and egg in a bowl and mix well. Fold in the blueberries. Spread evenly over the bottom of an 8-inch square pan.

For the **TOPPING**, combine the sugar, flour and cinnamon in a bowl and mix well. Cut in the butter until the mixture is crumbly. Sprinkle over the filling.

Bake at 375 degrees for 45 to 55 minutes or until hot and bubbly.

Yield: 6 to 9 servings

ICED CINNAMON BUNDT CAKE

CAKE
1 package yellow cake mix
1 (4-ounce) package vanilla instant
   pudding mix
1/2 cup vegetable or canola oil
1 cup water
4 eggs
1 tablespoon vanilla extract

FILLING
1/4 cup packed brown sugar
2 tablespoons cinnamon
1/4 cup chopped nuts (optional)

GLAZE
1 cup confectioners' sugar
2 tablespoons milk

For the CAKE, combine the cake mix, pudding mix, oil, water, eggs and vanilla in a mixing bowl and mix well. Beat at high speed for 6 to 8 minutes.

For the FILLING, combine the brown sugar, cinnamon and nuts in a bowl and mix well.

Pour 1/3 of the cake batter into a greased bundt pan. Layer the filling and remaining batter 1/2 at a time over the batter. Bake at 350 degrees for 55 to 60 minutes or until the cake tests done. Cool in the pan for 8 to 10 minutes. Invert onto a serving plate. You may bake in an angel food cake pan for 45 to 50 minutes.

For the GLAZE, combine the confectioners' sugar and milk in a bowl and mix well. Spread over the cake.

Yield: 8 servings

PARADES—Everyone loves a parade! Every Memorial Day and Fourth of July, neighbors come out decked in red, white, and blue for the local parade. The fire trucks blare their sirens and the Little Leaguers march to the beat of the high school band. One of the most enduring parades around is the LaGrange Pet Parade, which has been held on the first Saturday of June for more than sixty years. In addition to marching bands and clowns, the Pet Parade features pet owners marching their costumed pets. Local folklore advises brides to plan their weddings during the parade because it never rains on the Pet Parade.

CRÈME SHERRY POPPY SEED CAKE

CAKE
1 package yellow cake mix
1 (4-ounce) package vanilla instant
   pudding mix
4 eggs
1 cup sour cream
1/2 cup vegetable oil
1/2 cup crème sherry
1/2 cup poppy seeds

GLAZE
1 cup confectioners' sugar
2 tablespoons sherry

For the **CAKE**, combine the cake mix, pudding mix, eggs, sour cream, oil and sherry in a mixing bowl and mix well. Beat at medium speed for 5 minutes. Stir in the poppy seeds. Pour into a greased bundt pan. Bake at 350 degrees for 50 minutes. Cool in the pan for 15 minutes. Invert onto a serving plate.

For the **GLAZE**, combine the confectioners' sugar and sherry in a bowl and mix well. Spread over the cake.

You may bake the cake in small loaf pans and reduce the baking time.

Yield: 8 servings

ASPARAGUS CREPES

CREPES
1/2 cup sifted all-purpose flour
1/2 teaspoon salt
Dash of nutmeg
1 1/2 teaspoons sugar
4 eggs, well beaten
1 1/4 cups milk
1/3 cup melted unsalted butter

SAUCE
1/2 cup (1 stick) unsalted butter
1/2 cup all-purpose flour
3/4 teaspoon salt
1/8 to 1/4 teaspoon pepper
4 cups milk
2 bundles cooked fresh asparagus spears
   (about 32 spears)
Melted butter
Salt and pepper to taste
1/4 teaspoon nutmeg
1 cup shredded sharp Cheddar cheese

For the **CREPES**, sift the flour, salt, nutmeg and sugar together. Combine the eggs and milk in a bowl and mix well. Add the sifted dry ingredients and mix until just blended; the batter may be slightly lumpy. Heat a 6-inch skillet. Add a small amount of the melted butter and swirl to coat the bottom of the skillet. Spoon 2 1/2 to 3 tablespoons batter into the skillet. Tip to cover the bottom. Cook for 1 minute or until the underside is golden. Turn the crepe and cook until the underside is golden. Place on waxed paper. Repeat with the remaining batter, stacking the crepes between sheets of waxed paper.

For the **SAUCE**, heat the butter in a heavy saucepan until melted. Stir in the flour, 3/4 teaspoon salt and 1/8 teaspoon pepper. Whisk in the milk gradually. Cook until thickened, stirring constantly. Pour a small amount of sauce into each of two shallow ovenproof baking dishes. Brush the asparagus with melted butter. Season with salt, pepper and nutmeg. Roll two asparagus spears in each crepe and place in the prepared baking dishes. Pour the remaining sauce over the crepes. Sprinkle with the cheese. You may chill the crepes, covered, at this point until ready to bake. Bake at 400 degrees for 30 minutes or until the sauce is hot and bubbly.

Yield: 16 crepes

CRUSTLESS WESTERN OMELET QUICHE

4 eggs, beaten
3/4 cup milk
6 tablespoons half-and-half
1/2 teaspoon salt
Dash of pepper
8 ounces Swiss cheese, shredded

2 1/2 tablespoons all-purpose flour
8 slices bacon, crisp-cooked, crumbled
1/4 cup chopped ham
1/4 cup chopped green bell pepper
1/3 cup chopped onion, or to taste

Combine the eggs, milk, half-and-half, salt and pepper in a bowl and mix well.

Toss the cheese with the flour in a separate bowl. Add the bacon, ham, bell pepper and onion and mix well. Pour in the egg mixture and mix well. Pour into a greased square 9-inch pan. Bake at 350 degrees for 60 minutes or until the eggs are firm.

Yield: 6 to 8 servings

CRUSTLESS ZUCCHINI QUICHE

Perfect for brunch or with a salad for a light summer dinner.

3 cups grated zucchini
1/2 cup shredded Cheddar cheese
1/2 cup biscuit mix
1/2 cup vegetable oil

1/2 teaspoon salt
1/2 teaspoon dried oregano
3 eggs

Combine the zucchini, cheese, biscuit mix, oil, salt, oregano and eggs in a bowl and mix well. Pour into a greased pie plate. Bake at 375 degrees for 30 minutes or until golden brown.

Yield: 6 to 8 servings

CANADIAN BACON AND CHEESE STRATA

8 eggs, lightly beaten
3 cups milk
1 teaspoon salt
2 dashes of pepper
2 teaspoons dry mustard
1 onion, chopped

1 green bell pepper, chopped
1 pound Canadian bacon, chopped
2 cups shredded sharp Cheddar cheese
4 cups seasoned croutons
   (about one 5- to 6-ounce package)

Combine the eggs, milk, salt, pepper and mustard in a bowl and mix well. Stir in the onion, bell pepper, bacon and cheese. Add the croutons and stir gently. Pour into a buttered 9×13-inch baking dish. Chill, covered, for 12 hours or longer.

Bake at 375 degrees for 50 to 60 minutes or until the eggs are set. Let stand for 5 to 10 minutes.

Yield: 6 to 8 servings

SUNRISE BREAKFAST STRATA

Serve a crowd with this hearty, rustic dish. Its savory flavors are sure to satisfy even the biggest appetites.

1/2 cup (1 stick) butter or margarine,
   at room temperature
25 slices (about) French bread,
   crusts removed
1 pound Cheddar cheese, shredded
1 pound Monterey Jack cheese, shredded
1 pound bacon, crisp-cooked, crumbled
1 pound spicy sausage, browned, crumbled

1 cup sliced fresh mushrooms
1/2 cup chopped onion
1 red bell pepper, finely chopped
14 eggs
2 cups half-and-half
1 teaspoon salt
1 teaspoon pepper
1/2 teaspoon paprika

Spread the butter over both sides of the bread slices. Layer the buttered bread slices, Cheddar cheese, Monterey Jack cheese, bacon and sausage half at a time in a buttered 9×13-inch baking dish. Sprinkle the mushrooms, onion and bell pepper over the top.

Beat the eggs, half-and-half, salt, pepper and paprika in a mixing bowl. Pour over the layered casserole. Chill, covered, for 24 hours. Bake at 350 degrees for 1 1/2 hours.

NOTE: It is important that this dish be assembled and refrigerated for 24 hours before baking.

Yield: 10 to 12 servings

CONTRIBUTORS

We would like to thank all of those who graciously submitted their treasured recipes for this cookbook. Without their support, this project would not have been possible.

Barb Achenbaum	Heidi Gleason	Donna Mittelstadt
Donna Ackerson	Joyce Goldman	Becky Moats
Devon Allen	Liz Gonzalez	Jan Monahan
Jacquelin Arnold	Jackie Gupta	Renee Turano Novelle
Amy Bailey	Amy Habeck	Karen Novy
Kim Beerbower	Cindy Haller	Cristen Orput
Nancee Biank	Jean Harper	Carol Oudsema
Diana Bilenko	Tracey Head	Jackie Paez-Goldman
Cathy Bjeldanes	Sarah Headrick	Patty Paez
Emma Bjeldanes	Denise Howe	Raquel Paez
Christine Blake	Kate Huffman	Ginny Perkins
Jill Bonfiglio	Margaret Hughes	Karla Pope
Gretchen Boules-Paarlberg	Rob Johnson	Doris Potter
Martha Bratt	Stacy Johnson	Julie Potts
Angela Buikema	Susan Johnson	Kathy Riddiford
Melissa Burek	Carla Kantola	Carolyn Riley
Beth Buzogany	Michelle Kapp	Sarah Rivera
Yvonne Cain	Denise Kavuliak	Margie Saran
Joan Fitzgerald Clopton	Heidi Keeling	Theresa Schabes
Paula Cochran	Sharon Keough	Lisa Seplak
Sue Cocke	Beth Kleis	Allison Shannon
Rosanne Cofoid	Cindy Klima	Pamela Shannon
Jennifer Couzens	Kristi Knapp	Marion Sherwood
Linda Davis	Melinda Kollross-Marco	Kathleen Siffermann
Rina Daw	Dianne Krieger	Ann Smith
Melissa Ehret	Pamela LaPlaca	Denise Thomas
Gale England	Susan Laney	Amy Thompson
Beth Eschenbach Lambert	Kimberly Leigh	Laura Tomassone
Katie Eschenbach	Katherine Lewis	Leah Torsberg
Shannon Eschenbach	Sayle Little	Danielle Tuck
Carolyn Excell	Jeannie Marinelli	Anne Utz
Denise Field	Courtney McCarthy	Emily VanHoutte
Raquel Flood	Megan McCleary	Courtney Waters
Sondra Fowler	K.C. McClure	Alice Waverley
Kathleen Fuller	Shelly McMillin	Tiffany White
Paula Fuller-Goss	Lisa McPherson	Susan Wilson
Toni Gentleman	Lisa McTigue	John Yurchak

RECIPE TESTERS

With appreciation to our generous testers who opened their kitchens and gave us invaluable input.

Donna Ackerson
Devon Allen
Tracy Anderson
Polly Ascher
Cathy Bjeldanes
Christine Blake
Jeanne Blauw
Martha Bratt
Angela Buikema
Beth Buzogany
Alix Chesno
Joan Fitzgerald Clopton
Stephanie Dillard
Marjorie Duerr
Christie Eddins

Katie Eschenbach
Tina Garmon
Toni Gentleman
Heidi Gleason
Elizabeth Gonzalez
Laurel Haarlow
Amy Habeck
Sarah Headrick
Anastasia Hinchsliff
Megan Hinchsliff
Denise Howe
Heidi Keeling
Kristi Knapp
Megan McCleary
Shelly McMillin
Lisa McTigue
Donna Mittelstadt
Becky Moats
Renee Turano Novelle
Karen Novy
Carol Oudsema
Mary Oudsema
Jackie Paez-Goldman
Kathy Riddiford

Margie Saran
Claudine Schramko
Lisa Seplak
Barbara Serpe
Courtney Stach
John Summy
Amy Thompson
Leah Torsberg
Danielle Tuck
Melanie Unell
Courtney Waters
Alice Waverley
Fiona Wheeler
Pat Wichmann
Jamie Wichmann

INDEX

LIFE IS *Delicious*

INDEX